SERMONS
to the

12

SERM⊕NS
to the

12

JUNG Y⊕UNG LEE

Abingdon Press
Nashville

SERMONS TO THE TWELVE

This book is printed on acid-free paper.

Library of Congress Cataloging-in-Publication Data

LEE, JUNG YOUNG
   Sermons to the twelve.
   1. United Methodist Church (U.S.)—Sermons.
   2. Methodist Church—Sermons.
   3. Sermons, American. I. Title.
   BX8333.L36S47   1988   252'.076   87-14529

ISBN 0-687-38001-4 (alk. paper)

Scripture quotations unless otherwise noted are from the Revised Standard Version of the Bible, copyrighted 1946, 1952 © 1971, 1973 by the Division of Christian Education of the National Council of the Chuches of Christ in the U.S.A., and are used by permission.

Scripture quotations noted GNB are from the *Good News Bible*, copyright © American Bible Society 1966, 1971, 1976.

The chapter "The Bamboo Tree" appeared previously in *Thanks*giving*, J. LaVon Kincaid, Sr., Editor, pp. 7-11. Copyright © 1984 by Discipleship Resources. Reproduced by permission.

The chapter "The Hope of Resurrection" is adapted from the author's article "The Resurrection Hope" which appeared in *Adult Leader*, March-April-May, 1984, © 1983, and used by permission of Graded Press.

MANUFACTURED BY THE PARTHENON PRESS AT
NASHVILLE, TENNESSEE, UNITED STATES OF AMERICA

In memory of my mother,
who loved me and led me to follow Christ

Preface

I still recall what my wife used to tell me: "I cannot understand you," she said. "Why do you have to drive two hundred miles to preach in a tiny church without getting any money? You are a fool!" Perhaps she was right. Distance did not matter, and money was not a concern of mine. All I wanted was to preach. I have been a fool for the sake of preaching. This, then, is a collection of sermons by this foolish preacher.

Although my favorite hymn is "In Christ There Is No East or West," my favorite theme for preaching has been "In Christ there is East in West." Asian presence in America gives a distinctive flavor to the life of our church. In this volume, I hope to add Asian spices in preaching ministry.

"The Bamboo Tree" was originally published in *Thanks*giving* by Discipleship Resources of The United Methodist Church. I have revised it in order to include it in this volume. "The Hope of Resurrection" is a revision of "The Resurrection Hope," which appeared in *Adult Leader* (March-May, 1984) by The United Methodist Publishing House. I am grateful to have permission to reprint these sermons.

I am deeply indebted to many persons. Initially, J. Calvin Kincaid referred me to Michael Williams, Director of

Sermons to the Twelve

Preaching Ministries at the Board of Discipleship of The United Methodist Church, who expressed his interest in my sermons. I am also grateful to Derrick Norman and Robert H. Conn of Abingdon Press. Without their enthusiasm and support, the publication of this book would not have been possible. Finally, I should not fail to recognize the assistance and cooperation given by my wife, Gy, and my two children, Sue and Jonathan.

JUNG YOUNG LEE
Easter 1987

Contents

1

Introduction

*P*reaching means the proclamation of God's good news to mankind. Jesus began his preaching with the good news that the kingdom of God is at hand. The apostles preached the good news that Jesus Christ died for our sins and was raised from the dead for our salvation. We too preach the good news that the early apostles preached. We preach the same message, in fact, but within a different context. If we notice closely the content of the preaching done by the early apostles, to be found in the Epistles and in the Acts of the Apostles, we will be truly convinced that they spoke out of their own deep conviction. The conviction so expressed is neither that of doctrinal adherence nor that of intellectual persuasion regarding their central beliefs, but is a conviction based upon their personal experience. Their preaching was primarily their testimony of the living Christ and the loving God in their midst. It was their own personal experience with Christ that urged them to proclaim the good news. To them their experience with Christ was the most precious gift from God. Without that experience their claim to apostleship was vain. Paul became the Apostle of Christ by his experience with Christ; his confrontation with the risen Christ was thus the seal of his discipleship. Indeed, the real power of his preaching came from his experience. However great his eloquence might have been, he would not really have been an apostle if he had not had the experience of meeting with Christ on the road to Damascus.

Preaching, therefore, is more than expounding the Scriptures, more than telling the story of Jesus, more than explaining the meanings of our beliefs, more than persuading people to accept Christianity intellectually and morally, more than sharing insights and knowledge of the Christian faith, and more than prophesying God's will to mankind. What, then, is preaching? Preaching, to me, is to give myself to the people whom I serve; it is the offering of myself.

What do I mean in saying that I give myself in my preaching? I give my real self to the people to whom I preach—a real self that includes more than my doctrinal confession, more than my understanding of the Christian faith, more even than my experience with Christ; it also includes my background, my actual life, and those real feelings that arise from the roots of my existence. I do not want just to speak the Christian language or to talk about the Christian experience; I want to tell everything about myself, my real self, as a testimony of God's love and care. What God has done to me through Christ is the good news. Through my preaching, the people who hear me should get right into my life. Through my preaching, I open myself to my people. I often talk about myself, so that people may come to know my true self. If my preaching does not open the door to the inner chamber of my real self, my preaching is not genuine. To me, genuine preaching is to reveal the secret of my own self to the people, so that they can come into my life. If I simply speak from my own mind or emotions without opening up my secret chamber, my preaching is like the hollow sound of a clanging gong. Preaching is uncovering my true self. It is not wrapping up the Christian faith in a package of beautiful ideas. Preaching is not presenting an elegant appearance before people. It is exposing my flesh and blood. Preaching is not an art; it is my meditation in which I reflect my real self. Therefore, preaching is meditation in speech and in gesture and in movement. In meditation I, my people, and the living Christ come together. In this moment my preaching becomes genuine.

It is easy to say what genuine preaching ought to be, but it is difficult to practice it. If the sermons collected in this volume contain even the slightest notion of what I am attempting to say about genuine preaching, I would be most gratified. Almost all of these sermons were preached to a small congregation (Concrete United Methodist Church) in North Dakota. There were only twelve people who regularly came to the church, although the actual members numbered fewer than ten. After I stopped preaching, the church was closed. In honor of these twelve people, I chose the title of this book. All these sermons were preached without any written notes. I wrote them down each Sunday only after I came home from the service.

I am an Asian-American whose roots are in Korea, and my preaching reflects my own cultural and personal background. Because I want to present myself in preaching, my preaching often becomes in effect my autobiography. I have tried to present myself as I have actually been—a person greatly blessed with a rich past. The greatest gifts that God has given me are the experiences of pain, loneliness, joy, sorrow, and struggle. In these experiences Christ has been my only reliable companion. That is why when I speak of my own experience in preaching, Christ is present. The presence of Christ is indeed the essence of my life, for "it is no longer I who live, but Christ who lives in me" (Galatians 2:20). Thus, when I share myself, I transmit Christ. And it is from this conviction that I have spoken here of my life and of my self in preaching.

2

The Dandelion

*Consider the lilies, how they grow;
they neither toil nor spin; yet I tell you, even Solomon in all his glory
was not arrayed like one of these.*

(Luke 12:27, 28)

"It is already spring," I said, while opening the front door. I almost felt the spring. The cold winter was gone, and the cosmic resurrection was already taking place outside. Through the storm door I watched events outside. Things were starting to live again. The front lawn was turning green. "What a beautiful lawn we have!" I thought to myself.

Suddenly, I discovered a yellow flower at the far corner of the front lawn. Unconsciously, I kicked the storm door. I opened it vigorously and dashed out into the yard with bare feet. I ran to the corner and picked the dandelion. I tried to pull it out roots and all, but it was broken loose. I held the dandelion in my hand and looked at it for a while. It was golden yellow, like the rising sun. "Why don't I like you?" I said to the dandelion. The dandelion smiled back at me. It did not say it, but I knew what it tried to tell me. In its smile was the cynical message: "You hate me because I represent you." I became so sad that I lost the courage to question anymore. I sat on the lawn under the warm spring sun and looked mindlessly at the lonely dandelion for some time. Gradually my mind was taken far away to my early childhood in Korea.

I used to live in a small farming village about fifty miles north of Pyongyang, the capital of North Korea. When the spring came, the first things I saw were the dandelions blooming all over the countryside. I used to like the bright yellow flowers. When I was a boy, I used to pick them one by one and hold them together in my hand. And then I brought them into my home and placed them in a cup filled with water. The yellow flowers helped to brighten our dark rooms.

In the early summer, when all other plants were beginning to produce their green leaves, the dandelion was already producing its seeds. The golden flowers changed to white like cotton in the midst of a green field. On my way home from the public school, I would sometimes pick one and put it close to my mouth and blow on it as hard as I could. Then I would see the white seeds fly up in the air and come down like parachutes. Most of the seeds came down nearby, but a few, driven by the wind, rose high up into the sky.

Among them was one brave seed that went farther away than the others. It summoned the courage to go as far as it could. It had faith that it could find a better place to live. Going up high into the sky, it floated like a cloud and flew over the mountains, crossed the rivers and ocean, and finally arrived on the great continent known as North America.

It was certainly a strange place for the dandelion seed when it landed in the beautiful front lawn of a house. The dandelion seed was so afraid to land there, but it had no choice. The wind had calmed down, and the seed could stay in the air no longer. The dandelion seed noticed that the green grasses were curious about its coming; they were somewhat excited at seeing something new. The dandelion seed was at first delighted with its reception.

However, when the dandelion seed started to settle down

by covering itself up with rich black soil, the grasses said: "You had better not settle here. As you know, this is only for us." The dandelion seed, when it heard them, thought they were joking. "You are not serious, are you?" it said. The dandelion thought that, since they had welcomed its coming, they should also welcome its settling down. The grass said: "We tell you the truth. You belong at the roadside, where many wild plants grow."

"But everyone has the right to live wherever it chooses. I don't understand." The dandelion spoke as if there were nothing wrong in living with the green grass. The final warning came from the grass: "When spring comes, you will know what we mean." Regardless of what the grass said, the dandelion seed settled in the front yard and covered itself with rich soil, preparing for the cold winter in a strange land.

The cold winter did not last too long. Soon the warmer sunlight began to melt down the dusty snow, and spring approached in the yard where the dandelion had settled down. While the grasses and trees in the yard were still sleeping, the dandelion was already working to root itself deeply into the soil, at the same time sending its sprouts up faster than any other plants. The dandelion worked harder and longer than any others, because it had to prove itself in the new place. By the time the other plants and grasses had started to come up from the ground, the dandelion already stood aloof above all the others. By the time they had started to sprout leaves, the dandelion had already produced a bright, golden, round flower, resembling the rising sun. The dandelion was so proud of its flower, the only flower in the whole yard. The dandelion did it, in fact, to brighten up the yard and please its owner.

When the owner came out into the yard and saw the dandelion flower, he did not appreciate it. Rather, he hated it. He said to himself, "I thought I weeded out all the dandelions last year, but there comes up a new one again." He then came all the way over to the corner and pulled the dandelion up. He wanted to pull out the roots, but the plant was embedded so deeply in the ground that it was broken instead; only half of its roots came out. The man who pulled out the dandelion was frustrated, but he decided to give up. Rather than dig further, he threw away the dandelion along the roadside. The grass, seeing what had happened to the dandelion, said: "We told you so last fall. You do not belong here. Go away!" But the dandelion said nothing. Half of its root was already taken away. It could not go anywhere.

In spite of what had happened to the dandelion, it did not lose faith in God, who had called it to settle in this land. "I must work harder than ever before," the dandelion said to itself. It worked and worked to grow its root back to full size and then to come up from the ground. Again, the dandelion did its best to produce a beautiful flower. This time it produced a better flower, thinking that the owner was not pleased with the first one. The dandelion had confidence that this time the owner would be pleased with its flower, which was not huge and bright. Nevertheless, the man was angrier at the flower than before. "I hate to see that dandelion again," he said to himself. He pulled it out, but he failed once more to take everything out; the root was broken again. The dandelion was greatly hurt but did not lose faith. It rooted itself deeper and deeper. The more it suffered, the more its root penetrated into the ground. Its faith was expressed in its root. The dandelion's faith became stronger and stronger as it faced the hardship of its existence. The faith that God had called it to dwell in this land gave it an indomitable courage to pursue its goal. Nothing could thwart its purpose.

In due course another springtime came to the place where the dandelion dwelt. During the wintertime the dandelion had done its best to strengthen its root. It came out really strong this time and did its best to produce the most splendid flower in the yard. The dandelion thought that the owner of the house would be pleased with its flower. But again, the owner came out and pulled it out. This time he said, "I hate to see this yellow color in my green yard." When the dandelion heard it, he finally realized that the reason the owner hated it was because of its yellow color. The dandelion therefore decided not to display its yellowness. "I will have to conform to the same color that the lawn has," the dandelion said to itself. In order to save itself and to please the owner, the dandelion no longer produced its flower. It stayed green, like the rest of the plants in the yard. In this way it was able to survive another year without being picked by the owner.

The dandelion survived, but it was not happy at all; it had lost the meaning of existence. The dandelion tried to change its appearance to be like the grass, but it was not possible. However much it wanted to become like the grass in the yard, it could not do so. The dandelion knew that it was different from the others, and it could not disguise itself to be different from its own nature. "I fool myself in trying to become like the grass. The grasses are not going to accept me as one of them," the dandelion thought.

During the long winter the dandelion thought and thought and finally decided to bring out its own true nature, which was yellowness. "Without a flower my life is not worth living," the dandelion thought. So as soon as the spring came again, the dandelion stretched its long and handsome stem up to the sky and produced its yellow and golden flower. "If I am allowed to live for a few weeks, I can produce hundreds of white seeds and send them off from here," the dandelion said to itself. This was the vision that the dandelion dreamed. But its dream ended with a dream. In the dream the man came out and took the flower in his hand. He was an Asian-American, a yellow man, who was also dreaming. In his dream he became the dandelion.

Suddenly, I heard a familiar voice, "Daddy, Daddy." It was my child's voice. I was brought back to present reality. I then

saw the yellow flower that I was holding in my hand. I looked
at it anew. It was no longer ugly; it was beautiful and
magnificent. "How beautiful, how beautiful!" I exclaimed to
myself. Instead of throwing it away, I brought it into my house
and put it in a plastic cup filled with fresh water. I placed it on
the dining table to brighten up the room. Like the golden sun,
the flower shined on in my house for a long time. Several days
later its head turned white. I took it outside, put it close to my
mouth, and blew it as hard as I could. The white seeds went
up high in the sky and began to fall down like parachutes all
over the rich green yards. "Let them live; let them live
anywhere they want to live. It is God's world, and they are
God's creatures," I said as I watched them.

3

Our Native Land

By the waters of Babylon, there we sat down and wept, when we remembered Zion. . . . If I forget you, O Jerusalem, let my right hand wither! Let my tongue cleave to the roof of my mouth, if I do not remember you, if I do not set Jerusalem above my highest joy!

(Psalm 137:1, 5-6)

I did not know how dear my native land was to me until I became a foreigner in this country. I had seen many Chinese immigrants in Korea, but I paid no attention to them. I treated them as if they were not much different from us. The Chinese immigrants had their own schools, teaching in their own language. I also saw the Chinese flag at the school yard whenever I passed by. At that time I did not know why they had their own school and displayed their own flag, but now I know: they needed to show their affection for their native land.

I forget about my native land when I am busy with my work or engrossed in my family life. When I have a party I forget everything. At such times I often act as if I am not a foreigner. I want to identify myself with the people native to this land. But when the party is over, I return to myself. When I am left alone, I have a chance to think of my situation. I feel the urge to return to my own past. Especially in the deep night I weep when I think of my homeland. I can then recall every bit of landscape in my hometown and the faces of everyone with whom I grew up. The small farm town in which I lived then becomes a paradise. If I ever have a chance to return there, I should want to reenact everything I did when I was a boy. I liked the mountains that surrounded the town. I loved the beautiful azalea flowers on the southern hill. I used to fish with a tiny net at the stream that flowed near the town. I recall the huge chestnut trees that our family used to have, under which I enjoyed gathering chestnuts in the fall. I also had many friends who were available at any time I needed them. My parents and my kinsmen were caring and loving people. Everyone in the town was a part of my life. I want to return and live there the way I used to, but I know that I cannot. I can only return to that past in memories. These past memories are precious, but they also make me sad. Whenever I have thought of my homeland, I have wept.

The Israelites also wept when they thought of their homeland. "By the waters of Babylon, there we sat down and wept, when we remembered Zion." When I read the 137th Psalm today, I knew why they wept. I knew why they could not sing in the foreign land; I knew why they could not forget their days in Jerusalem; I knew why they were so bitter toward the enemy who occupied their homeland. My homeland, on the other hand, is in Korea, where I can return. I am not a captive in this country, but I am a war refugee. It was the Korean War that led me to migrate to this country. I came to this country for a better living. The Jews, however, went to Babylon as captives. They suffered more than I did. They had a more intensive longing for their homeland than I do. Therefore, when I read this psalm, I am comforted. The psalm helps me overcome the pain of my longing for my homeland.

Why do I have such a nostalgia for my homeland? Is it because I am an Asian in America? I used to wonder whether the Europeans in this country have the same nostalgia that I have. I have a friend who came from Norway. He told me that he feels homesick occasionally, but that he is not bothered by it much. He misses his homeland, but not painfully enough to cry at night. Why, then, do I have a more intensive form of nostalgia than he does? Perhaps, I am more lonely than he is. Whenever I am alone, I sense the strong desire to return to my homeland. Loneliness comes from isolation, and I have often been isolated in this country because I am an alien. To be an alien means to be alienated from the native. My alienation creates isolation, and isolation in turn creates the sense of loneliness. What are the things that alienate me, then, and set me apart from the natives of this country?

I am an Asian in America. I know that my bone structure is different from that of Caucasians. I know that the color of my skin is different from theirs: I am yellow but they are white. I know that my eyes have a different shape, being small and slanted, while theirs are large and round. I know that my hair is black: most of them have hair that is not black. I have a round, flat face; but they have long, thin faces. I am short, but they are tall. My physical features alienate me from my Caucasian brothers and sisters. I look odd among the Caucasians who comprise 90 percent of the people in my town. Because I look odd, I am isolated. I also isolate myself from them, because I know that I am odd. My Norwegian friend does not have the physical oddness that I have, and he is thus less alien from the Caucasian Americans than I am. I know that I cannot change my physical makeup. I also know that I cannot change my race. I am an Asian, and I must suffer for what I am. Some Asians in this country have attempted to change their physical features by plastic surgery or by coloring their hair. They want to change their looks, because they know that their looks isolate them from the Caucasians who dominate our society. But their attempts have not done much to improve their appearance. I know that I am different.

Although this difference isolates me from most of the people in this country, I take it as God's gift to me. I often become shy because I am of a minority race, but I cannot help myself.

My isolation becomes evident when people ask me about my native country. "Where do you come from?" people often ask. I usually say, "I came from Ohio," because in fact I used to live in Ohio before I came to the present location in North Dakota. People usually are not satisfied with my answer. They ask, "Where were you before you lived in Ohio?" Then I say, "I know what you want. I am a Korean." Then they are satisfied. They think that I am an alien because of my appearance. They don't seem to be ready to accept me as an American. That attitude has led me to believe that I don't belong in this country. Many people also ask me, "When are you going back to your country?" When I answer that I have no intention of returning to my homeland, they usually say, "I see," and go away. "Am I an unwanted person in this country?" I often ask myself. Legally I am naturalized, but actually I am an alien in this country.

My isolation is also due to the errors in my use of the English language. English is not my mother tongue. People instantly notice that I am a foreigner when they hear my speech. I have tried in the past to improve my speaking and writing skills, but I know that I will never be able to speak and write like a "real" American. My lack of communication skills hinders my efforts to become a part of American society. That is why I sense such isolation and loneliness in American life. I cannot laugh the way Americans laugh. I cannot cry the way they do. I often miss the joke. I cannot catch all the humor of their remarks. I often totally isolate myself when I am the only one who does not respond to their humor. I often imitate the crowd, but my behavior is awkward.

I have also a different way of thinking and a different value system because I come from a different culture. I love tranquility more than excitement. I love nature more than man-created things. I like certain kinds of food and music that most Americans shun. Therefore, I live and work with Caucasians but I am not a part of their company. I am an alien. However much I may want to be a part of them and make this country my native land, I cannot surmount the feeling of alienation. There seems to be an invisible and impenetrable wall that divides me from the Caucasian people in my town. The sense of loneliness arising from this isolation induces an irresistible desire to return to my homeland, where the invisible wall does not exist.

Because of my intense nostalgia I have returned to my native country more than a few times. However, I have also found that the land where I grew up has changed substantially. The people with whom I grew up have changed in their ways. I have also noticed that I have changed in my own way too because of my life-style in America. I have become a stranger, an alien, in my land. The homeland which I dream of returning to is not the same land. I cannot go back to the past. I have come to realize that I have no homeland at all. I am not really a Korean, because I am an American; I am not really an American, because I am a Korean in America. In fact, I am a Korean-American, who is neither American nor Korean. The real homeland where I want to return does not exist in the world. It exists only in my mind. I am thus reminded of the title of a novel by Thomas Wolfe, *You Can't Go Home Again.*

Jesus was also an alien in his homeland. He came to his own home, but his own people did not receive him. He was alienated from the mainstream of Jewish tradition at the time. Those who represented the mainstream of Jewish society, such as the Pharisees, scribes, and Sadducees, did not accept Jesus. He was rejected by his own people; he was ranked with the outcasts; he was a stranger to his own religious tradition. He was not even welcomed by his hometown people. Even the birds of the air have their nests and the foxes their holes, but the Son of man does not have a place to lay his head. He did not have a native land in this world, for he was not of the world. His native land was the kingdom of God.

To become a Christian means to be a follower of Christ. This means that Christians must become aliens to this world; that is, they must live in the world outside their homeland. Christians must become aliens who are not attached to their homeland. They must be rejected by it as Jesus was rejected. They must be sojourners on the earth, for there is no permanent place there for them to stay. They are pilgrims on earth. The real homeland to which Christians want to return is not the one where they were born or grew up. It is not the country of Korea, Japan, China, or America. It is the kingdom of God or the heavenly kingdom. The real homeland is not of this world; it is depicted by the Garden of Eden, the first and primordial homeland of everyone, the visible symbol of the kingdom of heaven.

The real homeland for the Christian is not out there somewhere far away from this country. The kingdom of heaven is not over there across the ocean. It is here where God reigns over me. It is not in the long-ago past when I was a child, but is now. The presence of God is known to me in this moment, right now. Therefore, my real homeland is here and now, where I am with Christ. When God becomes my Father and I become his child, then and there it is the kingdom of heaven. The land where I dwell is God's land, and I become a brother to those who dwell in this land. In Christ the invisible wall of partition breaks down and the sense of alienation evaporates. There is then a true unity and oneness among all peoples regardless of their different races, cultures, and languages. This true homeland that I know is in the world but not of the world.

Therefore, let me not waste my time dreaming of the homeland that only exists in my memory. The real homeland is right here where I live with Christ. For when Jesus said that the kingdom of God is at hand, he meant that it is neither in the long-ago past nor in the future of the last days nor in some distant land; instead, it is right here and now. For me, this means that I must transform my longing for my homeland in Korea into a real passion of love for God, whose presence alone can create the true homeland for me here and now. May that transforming power work in me and in you through the grace of our Lord Jesus Christ. Amen.

4

The Bamboo Tree

*Have this mind among yourselves,
which is yours in Christ Jesus, who, though he was in the form of
God, did not count equality with God a thing to be grasped, but
emptied himself, taking the form of a servant, being born in the
likeness of men. And being found in human form he humbled
himself and became obedient unto death, even death on a cross.*

(Philippians 2:5-8)

I am an Asian-American. Because of my Asian background
I cannot help being attracted to anything peculiarly Asian in
nature. Whenever I see an Asian picture or Asian furniture or
anything that is Asian, I have to look at it twice before I pass it
by.

Among the many trees, the bamboo is special to Asians. It
is certainly special for me. Whenever I see a bamboo tree, I
cannot help admiring it. Because I like the bamboo tree, I
brought one with me several years ago all the way from
California to North Dakota. I placed it right next to the door,
where everyone could easily spot it. My American friends
have often come and remarked that the bamboo gives an
Oriental touch to my home. However, they are not especially
attracted to it. On the other hand, when my Asian friends

come and see the bamboo tree, almost all of them pay extra attention to it with great admiration.

I know that the bamboo means something special to Asians. Why is it? There are many beautiful trees besides the bamboo. Why does the bamboo express the ethos of the Asian people? Is it special because it is an evergreen tree? But the pine is also an evergreen. Why then is the bamboo different from all other trees? It is special, I think, because *it is hollow.* This emptiness makes the bamboo different from all other trees and gives it a special significance to Asians.

I do not know why or how the Oriental people have come to place such value on emptiness. For most Westerners emptiness means very little. But for Asians, emptiness is often more valuable than fullness.

It is said that, in working on a painting, the Oriental artist usually spends more time on and gives more attention to the allocation of empty space than to actual drawing. The harmony and tranquility so typical of Oriental art are often effected by the creative use of empty space. Likewise, the basic feature of an Oriental house is emptiness. If you look at the traditional Korean *ondol* room (which is heated from below) or Japanese *tatami* (straw mat) room, you do not see any tables or chairs in it. If the room is not empty, it is considered useless. Likewise, the value of a bowl or utensil comes from its emptiness. When the bowl is full, it is of no further use. Here, emptiness has more value than fullness.

One of the famous temples in Kyoto is the Ryo-an Temple. It is famous because of its nearly empty garden. In the garden you do not see anything but the white sand and several groups of rocks. Nevertheless, hundreds and hundreds of people visit the temple every day to stand there and meditate on the empty garden. Emptiness for Asians means more than nothing. It carries a positive value.

Emptiness also has a special significance in Christianity. According to Paul's Epistle to the Philippians, Christ emptied himself, taking the form of a servant and being born in the likeness of men. This *kenosis* doctrine is one of our finest descriptions of the incarnation of Christ. Christ emptied himself of his glory, the glory of being equal with God. He emptied himself of his power, the almighty power over all things. He emptied himself of his authority to rule the world. By emptying himself of the form of God, he was transformed into the form of a servant. This is the true meaning of the Incarnation, the radical transformaton of the divine into the human nature. This transformation is possible because Christ emptied himself totally. In other words, God became a man by emptying himself of his divine nature.

A master cannot become a servant unless he empties himself of the nature of being a master. This emptying process is essential for a radical transformation. Christ poured out his divine characteristics and was transformed into the lowest category of human existence, that is, into the form of a servant. To me this is the uniqueness of Christ and of the Christian faith. I have never heard of such a doctrine in any other religion in the world.

Although the Buddha is somewhat comparable to Jesus, he was never during his lifetime considered to be divine. It is true that the Buddha had to renounce all of the privileges of being a prince when he became a monk, a decision known as the Great Renunciation. However, he did not take the form of a servant. Rather, he was elevated to the priestly class (or Brahmans) from the ruling class (or Kshatryas) in Indian society. Christ is unique because he, by the self-emptying process, transformed himself from the highest of the divine nature to the lowest form of human being. By taking the form of a servant rather than of a master, he came to understand the agony of suffering humanity and to empathize with the poor, the oppressed, and the weak. This was then his way of saving the world to himself, and to God.

If you have never been a servant, you may not understand

fully what it means to be a servant. I have been perhaps fortunate in many ways for having had both the experience of being a master and that of being a servant. When I was about six years old, our home in Korea was still wealthy enough to have many servants. I had my own servant, who was a fifteen-year-old boy, whom I called *Daeji* or "Pig." Wherever I went, he had to come along, too. He had to do whatever I commanded him to do.

I remember very well one day when we went to a mountain not far away from our home. Seeing a beautiful flower on the top of a rugged cliff, I pointed at it and asked my servant to bring it to me. Climbing up the cliff was so dangerous that he almost lost his life. Yet, he had to bring me the flower because he was my servant. On another occasion I fell down on the playground and hurt myself. As a small boy I cried loudly as I was coming into the house. My father was angry at the servant and said, "What were you doing when my son fell down?" He was severely rebuked, but he dared not say a word.

Time passed fast. Soon the Second World War was over, and the Korean War had started. In December of 1950, I was among the many thousands of war refugees traveling toward the south. I never thought when I left home that I would travel all the way to South Korea. Without any money, I became a penniless refugee in South Korea. I had to beg for food to keep myself alive. I traveled all the way to Milyang City, about seventy miles north of Pusan. There I was taken into a wealthy home, where I was hired to be the servant of an old gentleman.

During the three months of my stay with this man, I found out what it meant to be a servant. I was the extension of his hands and legs. I had to do exactly and efficiently what my master told me to do. More than that, I had to do whatever he expected me to do. No matter how much I disagreed with him or how unhappy I was with my work, I could not say a single no to his demands. I was practically his possession. I became his thing, not a person. I did not have any rights of my own. My entire existence depended on him. If he had wanted to kill me, he certainly could have. I lived under the shadow of fear and uncertainty. My master demanded of me absolute obedience, obedience even to death.

During those days I recalled my servant, "Pig," of my younger days. I came to empathize with those who were oppressed. I learned how inhumane it is to be a servant. Christ became a servant and was obedient even to death, so that all might be liberated from their slavery to sin. To be a servant means to empty oneself of one's right to be a free person. Christ, pouring out his divinity, took the form of a servant to save the world. This is the essence of the Christian message that we are to proclaim.

Being a Christian means to become a servant of God. Therefore, we as Christians must empty ourselves, as Christ did. We need to empty our insides like the bamboo tree. Our minds and hearts are full of envy, jealousy, prejudice, arrogance, and self-pride. Unless we empty ourselves of these things, we cannot become the instruments of God.

Let me share a story which can help us understand the importance of emptying our minds. During the Meiji era in Japan (1868–1912), Nan-in was a well-known Zen master. One day a university professor visited him to inquire about meditation. As an Oriental custom the master served tea. He poured the cup full and then kept on pouring. The professor watched the overflowing cup and, greatly disturbed, said, "It is overfull. Stop pouring!"

"Like this cup," the master said, "you are full of your thoughts. How can I teach you meditation unless you empty your thoughts? Empty your cup!" If our minds and hearts are full of past memories, worries, and selfish desires, we cannot receive the Word of God. We cannot receive Christ unless we first empty ourselves. By emptying ourselves we can become the temple of the Holy Spirit.

We remember the Christmas story. There was no room for Jesus in Bethlehem. Every room was crowded, so Jesus was born in a manger. Like Bethlehem, our hearts and minds are crowded with our own thoughts and desires. We have to make room for Christ, so that he can be born again and again in us. Certainly, the bamboo is a symbol of Christmas. When we were in California, we used the bamboo rather than the pine as our Christmas tree. It was so meaningful to us, because the bamboo tree, being empty inside, represents the incarnation of Christ and the emptiness of our hearts and minds, where Christ is born at Christmas.

The bamboo is also known as the symbol of faithfulness, as the faithfulness of a minister to his king. Like other evergreen trees, the bamboo remains faithful and the same, even in the cold winter. Moreover, its emptiness is an expression of faith. Like the empty bowl carried by a beggar or a wandering monk, the empty person is totally dependent on the giver. In many Third World countries, beggars carrying empty bowls to receive food are a common sight. When I was begging for food during the Korean War, I did not even have an empty bowl to take with me. I had to stretch out my empty hands. I had to wait, wait, and wait, until my empty hands were filled with food.

To be a faithful Christian means to be like the beggar who stretches out his empty hands to God. Our attitude must always be that of the empty hand or the empty bowl, which God can fill with his love. Our faith is the empty vessel, while God's love is the overflowing content. Our emptying process is the life of faith. Every day we are asked to empty ourselves. Our Christian living is none other than the life of emptying—emptying for God.

As the bamboo tree grows, its inside becomes more hollow. Likewise, our inside has to be emptied more and more as we grow in Christian faith. We have to allow more room for Christ as we mature in the Christian life. As the bowl is useful because of its emptiness, we become useful to God when we empty ourselves. Our old selves have to be emptied, so that our new selves may be born with the presence of Christ in us. In this way we are born again and again as we empty ourselves each time. When we completely empty ouselves for Christ, we are united with him. Then he is in us and we in him. And we can say with Paul, "It is no longer I who live, but Christ who lives in me" (Galatians 2:20). Amen.

5

The Yoke

Come to me, all who labor and are heavy laden, and I will give you rest. Take my yoke upon you, and learn from me; for I am gentle and lowly in heart, and you will find rest for your souls. For my yoke is easy, and my burden is light.
(Matthew 11:28-30)

Jesus, addressing mostly farmers in the early days of his ministry, knew the importance of harnessing the oxen to the yoke for the cultivation of the land. It is almost impossible in this country to see yokes or oxen, for they have been completely replaced by machines in our time. Only in some of the Third World countries are oxen and yokes still used today for farming.

In early days two oxen were fastened together by a yoke, a wooden frame placed upon their necks so that they had to work together in the field. The yoke, therefore, often became the symbol of captivity and enslavement. Slaves were often kept under a yoke (I Timothy 6:1) of wood or iron. Jeroboam was put in charge of the forced labor of the house of Joseph (I Kings 11:28). The oppression of one nation by another was also known as the yoke of bondage (Jeremiah 27:8; 28:4). Breaking the yoke became the symbolic expression of liberation from slavery and oppression (Jeremiah 28:2).

Through the coming of Jesus the old yoke of slavery and oppression is broken and the new yoke of Christ, the yoke of grace, is given to us. The yoke of the law is replaced by the yoke of grace, and our yoke becomes his yoke. Thus he speaks of "*my* yoke," the yoke of grace and liberation.

Jesus is then the bearer of a yoke. When Jesus said, "Take my yoke upon you, and learn from me," he could hardly have meant to take off his yoke and put it on us. Rather, I am compelled to think that Jesus was asking us to bear the yoke that he is bearing, to bear it in tandem with himself. "My yoke" can be understood as "the yoke that I bear," rather than as "the yoke that I made for you." Christ is not the one who gives us a new yoke, but he makes the old new by bearing it himself. In other words, the old yoke of slavery becomes the new yoke of grace because he bears it. Christ is not the one who bears the yoke alone, nor the one who gives us his yoke. That is, he invites us to bear with him the yoke that he is bearing. He wants us to bear it together. By bearing the yoke together with him, the yoke becomes grace.

Christ is here represented by a cow and we by cows. Like the cow he is gentle and lowly in heart. In the East the cow is the symbol of meekness and gentleness. When a Westerner asked Mahatma Ghandi why the Hindus in India respect the cows, he said, "The cow represents nonviolence." The idea of nonviolence, or *ahimsa,* lies at the core of Hindu beliefs. Christ as symbolized by the cow represents nonviolence, gentleness, and patience. Christ so symbolized depicts the suffering servant. The cow that symbolizes Christ is not a cow wandering the streets of New Delhi but a yoked cow, a working and suffering cow. He pulls the plow to cultivate the souls of men and women. He invites us to bear the yoke together for the work of redemption.

"Come to me, all who labor and are heavy laden" is Christ's invitation. He wants us to bear the yoke with him; he wants to make our yoke a part of his; he wants to share our burden so that we can become a pair. He is willing to take the other end of the yoke that we would otherwise have to bear by ourselves. This means that we do not have to bear the yoke by ourselves. The yoke is, in fact, too heavy for us to bear by ourselves. When the burden is too heavy, we become the victims of our own labor, and we experience nothing but suffering. This is perhaps why the Buddha defined human existence in terms of suffering, for each individual has to bear his own yoke, as the Buddha saw it, without any assistance from others. One of the key teachings of the Buddha, which he proclaimed just before he died, is the famous dictum, "Be a lamp to yourself."

The privilege gained from being a Christian is to know that one need not bear the yoke alone. Christ becomes a partner in our labor, a co-worker and co-sufferer. He invites us to bear the yoke that he is himself already bearing on our behalf. Thus, his yoke is none other than our yoke that he is bearing for us. Because he bears the yoke that we bear, it is light and our burden becomes easy.

When I was a boy in Korea, people used to go to an outdoor market, about five miles from our village, where they could exchange goods. Early one morning I had to carry on my back with an A-frame carrier a bag of rice weighing about seventy pounds. When I reached a point about halfway to the outdoor market, I was so exhausted that I could not hold up under the burden any more. Suddenly, then, the burden became light and I was released from exhaustion and suffering. Someone was helping me from behind! I turned and saw an old friend, who was following behind me and lending his hands to my burden. My yoke became easy and my burden became light. Thus, my walk to the market was transformed from a suffering journey into a joyful walk in fellowship.

The burden of our sin is too heavy to bear by ourselves. Therefore, Christ comes to bear it with us. He lightens the guilt of our sin and works to eliminate it altogether. He does not take away the sin or simply hand us the gift of salvation. I know that the idea of atonement or salvation that I am suggesting is radically different from the traditional concept. To think, however, in terms of the yoke that Christ bears together with us should help us to redefine the idea of salvation and redemption. Christ becomes our co-worker in the process of salvation. He is still working with us for our salvation. If the cross represents the initial event of salvation, the yoke represents its continuing process.

The yoke suggests a new idea of grace. It does not lift off your burden entirely, but it lightens it. It does not eliminate our suffering from sin, but it helps us to suffer together with Christ. Grace means that Christ is with us and suffers with us. It implies the active presence of Christ as our yokefellow. Grace helps us endure the pain and suffering of the world. It does not eliminate them. Grace means that Christ becomes our partner and bears the burden with us. Because of grace, we cannot be independent. Thus, the yoke of grace presupposes the responsibility of law. The law is fulfilled by grace, rather than being replaced by grace.

The deeper implication of the yoke is one that deals with the union of man and God. The root meaning of yoke is identical with that of yoga, the means by which the human and the divine are joined. Yoga, associated with certain techniques of meditation, is of different types. The common understanding of yoga is closely akin to marga yoga or the path through works; that is, marga yoga is closely identified with the yoke of law or salvation through works. However, the yoke of Christ is more closely akin to bhakti yoga, the path that man takes to God through his devotion and love. Each yoga has its own characteristics, but is not independent of the other. Marga yoga presupposes bhakti yoga, just as the yoke of law presupposes the yoke of grace. Man can connect himself to God, because Christ first connects himself to us under the yoke. Recognizing that Christ bears the same yoke that we bear, we are united with him. And by uniting with him in the yoke, we are also united with God. Through the yoke our work is connected with Christ, just as Christ's work is connected to us. In this way Christ shares his saving activities in the world, and in return our own works are gradually transformed into saving efficacies.

The yoke of Christ then serves as the symbol of mediation. Christ becomes the mediator through the yoke, for the yoke that he bears connects to the Father, as it connects to us. His connection with his Father is clearly expressed in the saying that Christ pronounced just before he asked us to bear his yoke: "All things have been delivered to me by my Father; and no one knows the Son except the Father, and no one knows the Father except the Son and any one to whom the Son chooses to reveal him" (Matthew 11:27). The connecting yoke that extends between Son and Father seems to be unique and unknown to us. This invisible yoke that unites both Son and Father is manifest only in part as we work together with Christ. As we become more and more involved in Christ and share the burden together, we are united with him. By uniting with him we will in turn be united with God through the yoke of Christ. And finally, when we become united with God through the yoke, we also become his co-workers in the process of building his kingdom on earth.

Christ calls us to realize that he is bearing the yoke that we bear. He is symbolized by the cow, which bears the burden of our work. He is then the suffering servant who bears the sins of others that he has not committed himself. He volunteers to bear the other end of our yoke, so that our burden becomes light. When he takes my yoke, it becomes his yoke; and I bear his yoke in return. This is the true meaning of grace. God through Christ comes first to bear our burden, so that our burden becomes his also. In this way God works in us and through us. The yoke connects us to God, just as he connects to us. To become a Christian means to bear the yoke of

Christ. It means to be a fellow worker with Christ. In Paul's words, as a "true yokefellow" (Philippians 4:3), a fellow worker with Christ, we are reminded of the fact that we are not alone. Christ is with us and bears the burden that we bear. He suffers with us when we suffer, and works with us to cultivate our souls. That is the meaning of the yoke. It is the yoke of grace, unity, and peace. Amen.

6

Light

In him was life, and the life was the light of men. The light shines in the darkness, and the darkness has not overcome it.

(John 1:4, 5)

Light is often taken for granted in our life, because it always exists. The significance of light is known only when we have lost our sight or have been kept out of the light. Think of yourself as blinded or as living underground! How precious the light would be in your life! Life without light is not worth living.

In the Bible the Word, representing Christ, is identified with light. Thus, Jesus said, "I am the light of the world" (John 8:12). His light is intended to shine in our lives; but all too often the light is hidden because of sin, which, like a cloud, prevents the light from shining. In truth, light shines always as the sun shines in the day; but we hide ourselves from it because of our sins.

Light is the source of life. It nourishes the plants so they can grow. It helps reveal the various forms and orders of existence. Light provides us with a sense of security when we fear the darkness and with hope when we shrink from the uncertainties of life. Christ is the light that shines in the world.

First of all, light is the primordial source of life and creativity. As we all know, no independent plant life can grow without light. Along with the light comes the warmth that germinates the seed. It is then the light that sustains new life. The plant can grow by light through the process known as photosynthesis. Light, in this respect, is a primordial element of life. Life not only evolves but produces itself through the light. Light is essential in order for the plant to bear fruit.

A few years ago I bought a tomato plant by mail order. The plant was supposed to bear tomatoes inside the house. However, it did not bear tomatoes in spite of its maturity. I later found out that it needed more light in order to yield its fruit. Thus, light is essential not only for growth but also for the fruitage of a plant.

In the story of Creation, light is given first priority in the process. God first created light: "Let there be light" (Genesis 1:3). And all other things were created afterwards. The separation of light from darkness was then the second act of God's creative process.

A similar phenomenon is also depicted in the Chinese book of cosmology, the classical *Book of Changes* or the *I Ching*. In this book the first element or the first hexagram is the symbol of great yang or pure light, consisting of six yang lines. The second element or the second hexagram is the symbol of great yin or pure darkness, consisting of six yin lines. Yang, the symbol of light, represents the creative power, while yin, the symbol of darkness, represents the receptive power that complements the creative power. In the *Book of Changes* the combination of yin and yang, or darkness and light, comprises not only the beginning of all other things but the basis for them all as well. In other words, the combination of the first and second elements (hexagrams) produces sixty-four elements (hexagrams), which represent everything in the world. Thus light, the first element in the creative process, is the prime agent of all creative activities.

Light is creative not only in the physical world but in the spiritual world as well. It was light that changed the life of Saul, who saw the light on his way to Damascus. The light that struck him was an inner light, representing Christ, who said, "I am the light of the world." Christ came to Saul as the light, and Saul ("who is also called Paul") became a new person through this light. Before the light Saul was the enemy of Christ, but after the light he became an ardent and faithful follower of Christ. Thus, it was the light that transformed his life and created him a new person out of the old.

Second, light reveals truth, righteousness, and beauty. Light helps reveal the righteous order of God's creation, while darkness is closely connected with moral chaos. There is no order to be found in darkness. We remember very well the time when New York City was completely blacked out. During the time of blackout, law and order in the city were gone. Many licentious activities, such as lewd acts, rapes, thefts, and murders, took place because there was no light. Light helps bring order and law back from chaos. Without light neither is the law enforceable, nor order discernible.

Light also reveals truth. Without light truth cannot manifest itself. True fact and falsity cannot be distinguished without light. In the *Republic,* Plato attempted to illustrate the discrimination of false perception from the true through the "Allegory of the Cave." Those who dwell in the cave and are thus in darkness are unable to understand the truth, for truth reveals itself in the light. Likewise in Christian thought, since truth is known only in the light, Christ—who represents the truth—is also light. Christ as truth reveals himself to us in the light, but we still love the darkness and are fond of illusion. In a way we are similar to the cave dwellers. "The light shines in the darkness, and the darkness has not overcome it." By the light of Christ we would be enlightened. Then when we are enlightened, we can really see truth as we ought to see it. To see light, therefore, when we have been engulfed in darkness, means to be enlightened and to be awakened from dreams. Through the grace of God we can open our eyes to see the shining light of Christ.

Light also reveals the beauty of the world. No beauty in darkness! During the Korean War, in 1950, I stayed underground for three months. There was no light there; I could not see anything in this place. Of course, there was no beauty whatsoever. But the beauty of the world burst forth when I finally got out of the underground place on an early October morning. It was the first time I had seen the light in three months. The light was so bright that I could not open my eyes for some time. I gradually opened them, however, and then saw the world in which I was now living. I saw the marvelous beauty of the world that God had created. I saw the blue autumn sky infinitely extended, the small yellow pumpkin flower on the hedge, and the falling leaves glaring in the sun. I touched the lonely pumpkin flower delicately with my fingers to sense its pulse. I heard the sound of rustling branches and bouncing leaves on the ground, which gave me a sense of being lifted up into infinite space. I also saw the blades of grass, so mysteriously shaped. Every blade was unique to me in its own way. Everything in the world was so beautiful that I had no words to express it. In mystic transformation, I felt that the world was so transparent that I was infinitely extended so as to touch every corner of the universe. The air was so fresh that I felt almost as though a flush of cold water was passing through my lungs to cleanse them. I could find no words to express the beauty of the world; I simply said a few times, "How beautiful! How beautiful!" That moment, even though a drop in time, was infinite in depth and height. The beauty of the world provided me with a sense of rapture that I had never experienced before. And it was the light that revealed the true beauty of the world. When, emerging from the darkness, I saw the marvelous light, I also saw the unspeakable beauty of the world. Light reveals beauty, as it also reveals the truth and righteousness of God. To live in Christ means, then, to discover the true beauty of the world, for Christ is the light of the world.

Finally, light is the hope of the world. While darkness is associated with disappointment, light is the symbol of hope. In the dark moments of our life, light can guide us into the future.

When I was a boy, I had to go into the mountains to gather firewood. We had no electricity or gas for heating our home or cooking meals in those days. Instead, we had to gather enough firewood for the cold winter season. During the autumn months the young people in my town were kept busy gathering firewood. One day I decided to join them in their trip to the mountains. I happened to be the youngest among them and the most inexperienced worker. Since most of the firewood had already been taken from the nearby mountains, we had to go farther away from town. I cannot recall how far we went, but we must have been about ten miles from home when we came upon plenty of firewood on a rugged mountain. By the time we had gathered enough firewood and were ready to leave for home, it had gotten late. The sun had already set in the west, and darkness was spreading fast, already covering the lower valleys amid the mountains. Everyone was hastening to get back home. Since I was the last and had the heavy load, I kept getting farther and farther behind the group. Soon I was too far behind, and finally, I lost the way. I yelled at them to wait for me, but all that I heard was my own voice echoing back to me from the deep mountain recesses. I began to hear the cries of wolf and wildcat. I did my best to get out of the mountains, but it was useless. Finally I gave up and threw away the firewood I had gathered. I decided to rest on a huge rock, for it was now too dark to find my way home. Suddenly I saw a light blinking from far away. The light gave me hope. It restored my courage and strength to go forward in the direction from which the light was shining. Finally, I found a tiny house, where I was allowed to spend the night.

Whenever I recall that experience, I can easily interpret the light as a sign of hope in darkness. It was that blinking light that gave me hope. Christ is the light that gives hope to all mankind. He is the blinking light to lost travelers in the mountains. He is like a lighthouse to the weary, struggling, lost sailors on the sea. Christ is present like the light of the sun to rescue all lost souls.

Today we are faced with uncertainties and fears. It is a dark moment in history. The fear of an imminent nuclear holocaust, the breakdown of family life, increasing disorder and theft, domestic and social violence, the widening gap between the rich and the poor, and the growing tension between East and West constantly threaten the very existence of our civilization. In this dim moment of history we find hope in Christ, who shines like the morning star in the darkness of human history. In our personal life Christ is the light of our souls shining in the shadow cast by fear and distrust. Christ is our hope, for he is the light of the world. Let his light shine in our darkness. Amen.

7

The Living Water

Jesus said to her, "Every one who drinks of this water will thirst again, but whoever drinks of the water that I shall give him will never thirst; the water that I shall give him will become in him a spring of water welling up to eternal life." The woman said to him, "Sir, give me this water, that I may not thirst, nor come here to draw."

(John 4:13-15)

Just as light is the prime principle of creativity, so also water represents the reverse side of the creative principle. Water is the background of life and creation. Light cannot act on behalf of life without water. Light is important in the life process because of water. Without water, light destroys life. As we learn from the story of Creation in the Old Testament, water serves as the background of life. The first of all living creatures were those in the sea. Birds came, and then the animals that creep upon earth came next. We also know that our own body cannot survive without water. Our body consists of more water than of any other substance. If light is the positive principle, then water represents the negative principle in creation. The Eastern people, especially the Chinese and Korean people, call the positive principle yang and the negative principle yin. Yang is then the symbol of light, male, heaven, and spirit; and yin is the symbol of water, female, earth, and matter. These two primordial symbols, yin and yang, have been regarded as the essence of all things. Yin and yang are united together in the processes of creation and procreation. Water is more than a background for the creative process. It is the symbol of purification and renewal. Water is used in baptism to symbolize the washing away of our sins. Purification is essential for renewal. The new creation presupposes the end of old creation. Thus Paul said, "The old has passed away, behold, the new has come" (II Corinthians 5:17).

In the passage of John 4:7-15, Jesus was no doubt thirsty after a long journey with his disciples. When his disciples went into a town to gather food, Jesus went to the well of Jacob and asked a Samaritan woman for water. Their conversation on the subject of water soon focused upon the spiritual message of the living water.

First of all, the message stresses the importance of being thirsty for the living water. If you have never been thirsty, you will not understand how painful it is to be without water. You may have read stories of journeys through the desert where water is not easily found. After many days of travel without water, finding an oasis must be a real joy. Although I have never been in a desert, I did experience a condition of real thirst during the Korean War. Not only was the area we were in completely destroyed by bombing, but the drinking water was poisoned by the withdrawing armies. For almost two days the people had searched for drinking water. It was almost impossible to find any water that was not contaminated by chemicals. After three days without water, we finally arrived at a green hill, where we found a tiny spring of water coming from between two huge rocks. Everyone was so excited to see the water. We were even relieved just by looking at it. The unbearable pain of thirst was gone immediately when we tasted the living water. Through this experience I came to know how precious drinking water is, although we take it for granted when we are not thirsty.

Psalm 42 says, "As a hart longs for flowing streams, so longs my soul for thee, O God. My soul thirsts for God, for the living God." Just as our thirsty body craves water, so should our soul search for God. Unless our soul thirsts, we cannot seek God. When we are thirsty, we are so desperate for water that we seek nothing else. Likewise, when our soul is thirsty, we become so desperate that our whole self longs for God. Wherever we are and whatever we do, we have to think of water when we are thirsty. In the same way, when our soul thirsts we must give up everything in search of God.

This kind of passionate search for God seems essential if we are to find him. I knew a Korean woman who had been in my congregation. She told me that she almost killed herself when she could not find Christ. She said: "I felt that my life was worthless without finding Christ. My mind was completely preoccupied with my longing for him. I would have killed myself if I had not found him at the very last moment. Then I saw someone putting his hand on my head. I knew that he was Christ." She was not sure whether this experience was real or only a dream, but she felt that she had received a new life from it. There are countless stories about the intense longing for God. A Hindu saint, Ramakrishna, who, after years of devotion to his god, Kali, failed to find her revelation, finally resolved to stick his sword into his throat as a sign of his absolute devotion to his god. At that very moment Kali revealed herself to him. He was truly thirsty for Kali's revelation.

A religious attitude toward God should be the condition of our thirst. The thirstier we are, the more we appreciate the drinking water. Likewise, the more intense our search for God, the more appreciative we are when we come to know God. When we are really thirsty, the water tastes unusually good. When we are not thirsty, however, the water is not needed. Our religious life is similar. God is present everywhere, but our experience of God is different. If our soul is really thirsty for him, our experience is great. If our soul is not thirsty for him, we may not experience his presence in our lives at all. When we are not thirsty, plain water seems tasteless to us, and we want something extra, like a soft drink. Likewise, when we are not thirsty for God, our religious life is dull. We have to make religion interesting in order to attract people to God. The essential presupposition of the religious life, therefore, is the condition that the soul be thirsty for God.

The living water that Jesus speaks of here is more than just water. It is the symbol of Christ. Jesus said, "Whoever drinks of the water that I shall give him will never thirst; the water that I shall give him will become in him a spring of water welling up to eternal life." In response to this, the woman said, "Sir, give me this water, that I may not thirst, nor come here to draw." Here, the water seems to represent the Word which became flesh and dwelt among us. In other words, the living water represents the spiritual presence of Christ. The spirit of Christ is identified with the spring of living water. The water is living because it is connected with the spring that produces water. If the presence of the living Christ is to be identified with the spring, then we will be cleansed and renewed continually by the presence of Christ in us. The spring of water flows ceaselessly to those who are poor, helpless, and weak. It renews their strength as the spring renews that of the thirsty people. Anyone who drinks of this spring of water will thirst no more, for the spring is the eternal source of water.

A spring of water creates a sort of well. In earlier days the community was formed around a well. In my own early days the small farm town where I grew up was formed around a well-known spring, which even severe drought had never dried up. A public well was built around the spring. Everyone in town came to draw water from this well. The spring of water in this well then became the source of life for the town. Everyone had to have water from this well. Moreover, the well became the focal point or gathering place for the townspeople. Especially women came not only to draw water from the well but to wash clothes and to quench their thirst. It became the center of their community life.

The presence of Christ can be easily compared to this well. Everyone needs Christ as the source of renewal. Like the spring of water, the presence of Christ in us renews our soul again and again. Paul said that in Christ we are new creations. Moreover, the presence of Christ, like the well, is the focal point of our Christian community. Our community life is centered around the presence of Christ, who draws the people together for refreshment as the well does. Christ should occupy the center of our lives, as does the well in the community. He should become like "the spring of water welling up to eternal life."

The living water of Christ should penetrate into every corner of the world, so that the kingdom of God may come upon earth as it is in heaven. Everyone, therefore, should respond to Jesus in the same way that the woman at the well did: "Sir, give me this water, that I may not thirst, nor come here to draw."

We should not let ourselves be cut off from Christ, the source of the living water. For if we do, we will turn out to be dead persons, just as any water that is cut off from the spring is dead water. Alan Watts, who interpreted Zen Buddhism to the West, once said that any water taken into a bucket from a stream is dead water. Inside the bucket the water is cut off from the flowing brook. It is not connected with the source, with the spring that constantly produces new water. The water in the bucket, therefore, is dead. It contaminates itself. When we are cut off from the presence of Christ, who is the source of our renewal and purification, we too contaminate ourselves; our sin grows, and eventually our greed and selfish desires will take control of our body. We should not become like the water in the bucket. Instead, let the spring of water that is in us clean, refresh, and renew our lives. To have that spring of water in us, we need to have a soul that thirsts after God. Amen.

8

The Hope of Resurrection

*D*on't be alarmed," he said. "I *know you are looking for Jesus of Nazareth, who was crucified. He is not here—he has been raised! Look, here is the place where he was placed. Now go and give this message to his disciples, including Peter: 'He is going to Galilee ahead of you; there you will see him, just as he told you.' " So they went out and ran from the tomb, distressed and terrified. They said nothing to anyone, because they were afraid.*

(Mark 16:6-8 GNB)

Death is the inevitable finale of life and represents the symbolic extinction of our existence. As soon as a baby is born, he begins the journey toward death. The longer we live, the closer we sense the presence of death. No matter how successful we might be in life, how much money we may gain, or how famous we might become, we are powerless before death. Death destroys for us everything we have accumulated in life. That is why we associate death with tragedy and the utter disappointment of human hope. Yet without death there can be no hope of resurrection.

The crucifixion seemed to mark the end of the disciples' hopes and aspirations for the establishment of the kingdom of God on earth. The death of Jesus meant the end of everything that they had hoped for: a seat at his right hand when the kingdom was established, or perhaps a throne from which to rule over the twelve tribes of Israel. Their ambition was not too different from ours. They were, no doubt, proud to be closely associated with such an important person. After all, they had "front row seats" that enabled them to see Jesus' miracles and hear his teachings. Being the disciples of Jesus during his few years of ministry must have been an exciting experience. After being a part of these happenings, however, it was shattering for them to witness his death. All their aspirations and dreams died, and they were left devoid of hope.

However, something miraculous happened. Jesus was resurrected from the dead! According to Mark 16:1-8, Mary Magdalene, Mary the mother of James, and Salome went to the tomb on the third day after the death of Jesus to complete the rites of burial. When they arrived, however, they found that the stone was already rolled away, and instead of finding the body of Jesus inside, they saw a young man in a white robe who must have been a heavenly messenger. He said to them, "Don't be alarmed. . . . I know you are looking for Jesus of Nazareth, who was crucified. He is not here—he has been raised! Look, here is the place where he was placed. Now go and give this message to his disciples, including Peter: 'He is going to Galilee ahead of you; there you will see him, just as he told you' " (GNB). The women were terrified and ran away trembling. Because of their fear they did not tell anyone.

We should ask ourselves whether we are like those women who were afraid to speak out about the resurrection of Jesus. In a way, many of us are; often we are afraid to speak out about Christ's resurrection, not because of a terrifying experience, but because we do not want to look foolish by telling of something that seems unscientific and unintelligent. We are not here arguing the authenticity of the witnesses but our conviction and faith in the New Testament witness of the resurrection of Jesus. Without a strong conviction we can become timid and easily avoid the topic of the resurrection.

Suppose that we were the witnesses at the empty tomb. What would we have done? Perhaps we would also have been terrified and run away as fast as we could. However, we should not have kept the story to ourselves. We should have told everyone we met about such an astonishing event.

The story of the first Easter reminds me of an experience I had when I was a young student in Korea. In those days only a small number of students were allowed to attend high school. The high school entrance examination was, in fact, so competitive that only one out of fifty applicants passed. When I took the examination, I never thought I would make it. However, when I went to see the results on the announcement day, I was amazed to find my number (the number given to me at the time of the examination) on the long white sheet hung on the wall of the school building. "I passed it!" I almost shouted with joy. I was so overwhelmed that I ran all the way home without stopping—more than ten miles. I wanted to tell my parents before I told anyone else. As soon as I reached home, I cried out, "I passed the exam! I passed the exam!" When my parents heard the news, they embraced my sweaty and exhausted body, sharing my joy. I was so overwhelmed with joy that I had to tell others as well. I went out and told everyone that I met. Some of them did not pay any attention to what I said. They did not even know what it meant to pass the high school entrance examination. I, no doubt, appeared foolish to them.

In the same manner, had we been witnesses to the Resurrection, we would probably have become as fools. We would have felt compelled to speak out wherever we went and to whomever we met.

The disciples did just that. The Resurrection restored their faith, and they were given a new and stronger hope for the future. They recalled what Jesus had said: "The Son of man will be delivered to the chief priests and scribes, and they will condemn him to death, and deliver him to the Gentiles to be mocked and scourged and crucified, and he will be raised on the third day" (Matthew 20:18*b*-19). The Resurrection became the seal of their faith and the foundation of their hope. They were emboldened to preach the resurrection of Christ.

The central message of the Acts of the Apostles is the Resurrection: "Jesus is risen!" This news was not accepted with enthusiasm by everyone and eventually brought the apostles to trial. Paul said to Felix, the Roman governor, "With respect to the resurrection of the dead I am on trial before you this day" (Acts 24:21). The power of that message also brought people together to form the church. Those who were witnesses of the Resurrection had to proclaim it. They did not question how or in what manner Jesus was raised; they simply proclaimed that "Jesus is risen!"

Soon, however, those who had not witnessed the Resurrection began to question the reality of the event. How could a dead person be raised after three days? The body would have begun to decay by that time. All kinds of questions began to be raised by those who had only heard about the resurrection of Christ. We have the record of a classic case in the Corinthian community. Paul took the entire fifteenth chapter of his first letter to the Corinthians to deal with the question of the Resurrection. For Paul, the Resurrection was the key to the entire preaching or *Kerygma.* If Christ was not raised, then faith is in vain and we have nothing to preach. Paul tried to explain it as intelligently as he could, although resurrection cannot be totally explained in human terms. One thing that Paul made clear in I Corinthians 15 is that the life of the resurrection is not the same as the life before resurrection. The life before resurrection is that of the mortal or physical body, whereas life after resurrection is that of the immortal or spiritual body that liberates a person from earthly limitations. The quality of life seems to alter after resurrection. Resurrection is neither the continuation of our earthly life nor the unending postponement of death. Resurrection yields a new form of life. Because of this qualitative difference between the life of resurrection and the life of this world, we cannot fully explain the mystery of Christ's resurrection and the empty tomb.

When I was a boy, my mother used to raise silkworms in our country home. Tiny silkworm eggs were hatched in a small container on the warm *ondol* floor (the floor was heated from below). When the eggs were hatched, the tiny worms were fed mulberry leaves. The worms gradually grew and, after a few months, filled our living room. When their bodies began to change from a greenish to a yellowish color, pine branches were brought in and placed over them so they could climb onto the branches and spin their cocoons. The cocoons were so beautiful that I decided to keep one in my room. One day I discovered a big butterfly coming out of the cocoon, and saw it fly up to the ceiling. I was amazed at this experience. I could not quite figure out where this beautiful butterfly had come from. I could not understand how an ugly silkworm, which I thought was dead, had changed into a beautiful butterfly.

When I think of the empty tomb of the Gospels, I think of the empty cocoon of my childhood. Resurrection can be compared to the transformation of silkworms into beautiful butterflies. Caterpillars are not able to think of themselves as flying. They do not even know how to run. How could ugly, crawling worms conceive of themselves as beautiful butterflies? There is a qualitative difference between the lives of caterpillars and those of butterflies. However much the caterpillars might want to know how it feels to fly, they have only the experience of crawling. Only when the caterpillars become butterflies do they know what it means to be a butterfly. This transformation is a reality that is known only by experience. Similarly, however much we try to understand resurrection, we will never understand it until we experience it. Those who witnessed the resurrection of Christ proclaimed what they had seen and experienced. They had to become as fools in the eyes of unbelievers. In reality they were not fools, for they proclaimd what they had seen. The story of the empty tomb comes alive and the appearance of the resurrected Jesus becomes real in our lives when we admit our limitations. Any attempt to explain this mystery in human terms only reduces it to less than reality.

What is asked of us as Christians is to witness to Jesus' resurrection. We must not keep it to ourselves because of our fear of appearing foolish. we must run, run all the way, even to the end of the world, because the proclamation of this message is the urgent task of the church. This message is a message of the hope of resurrection for everyone. May this hope be part of your hope! Amen.

9

I Am the Prodigal Son

So he got up and started back to his father. He was still a long way from home when his father saw him; his heart was filled with pity, and he ran, threw his arms around his son, and kissed him. "Father," the son said, "I have sinned against God and against you. I am no longer fit to be called your son." But the father called to his servants. "Hurry!" he said. "Bring the best robe and put it on him. Put a ring on his finger and shoes on his feet. Then go and get the prize calf and kill it, and let us celebrate with a feast! For this son of mine was dead, but now he is alive; he was lost, but now he has been found." And so the feasting began.

(Luke 15:20-24 GNB)

The story of the prodigal son is one of the most beautiful tales found in the Bible. The story itself bears a message that conveys a universal aspect of human experience. Most of us have had experiences somewhat similar to that of the prodigal son. Although our experiences may have been somewhat different from those of the Bible story because of different circumstances and times, we can each of us easily identify with the prodigal son. I can tell many stories similar to that of the prodigal son. Let me share with you one of the stories that helps me understand the real meaning of the prodigal son in the Bible.

My story takes place in 1950, when I was a teenaged boy. Since my family was very poor after the Land Reform Act in North Korea, I was not given a chance to go to high school. My home was in a remote farm village far from any large city. Thus, instead of going to a city high school, I decided to enter a technical training school for six months and get a job in a huge steel smelting company in Kangsu, about twenty miles north of Pyongyang, the capital of North Korea. I worked in the company for some time to establish a good reputation. I was, therefore, recommended by the company to go to Russia to study the steel industry. I was overwhelmed by the news. My friends gave me a farewell party before I left the company. I was filled with joy when I returned home. When my mother came out to greet me, I almost shouted, saying, "I am going to Russia! I am going to Russia!" My mother was somewhat disturbed with my joy. "What did you say, my son?" Her voice was rather sharp and cold. "I have been recommended to go to Russia to study." I was aghast at her unsympathetic attitude.

It took a long time to explain to her the opportunity I had won to go to Russia to study in a field in which good technicians were in demand in Korea. My mother was unhappy, however, at the prospect of my going to Russia. She insisted that I should stay close to her, for she needed me. I had sent her money that I had earned from my work at the factory. But she also felt that because I was one of the older children, it was my responsibility to take care of my younger brothers. Moreover, she simply did not want me to go away to a strange land. I tried very hard to convince her that I had to go to Russia. Like most young people, I wanted adventure. I also wanted to be free from my parents and from my small world in Korea. I thought of the opportunity to learn many different things from the Russians that I had never known before.

We argued all that evening. I knew that I had to yield to my mother, for in the traditional structure of Korean society she would have had the power of decision, even though this was not true in a Communist society. However, if I should go along with my mother's advice, I would lose too much in my life. Therefore, I felt compelled to go against my mother's will.

I arose early the next morning, thinking that she would not yet have awakened. But she was already awake. Approaching me, she said, "You really want to go." I nodded silently. "Let me cook your breakfast," my mother said as she entered the kitchen. I said: "No. My train leaves at seven o'clock. It is going to take at least an hour to get to the station."

She knew that I had to go, and she helped me to pack a few things in my bag. She came out all the way to the edge of our village to send me off. She stopped me for a moment and gave me some money that she had saved. Then she said; "Take this with you. Write me when you get there. Please come back soon. I will wait for you every day." I said, "Yes, Mother. Don't worry!" Embracing me with a last hug of farewell, she then let me go. I saw the tears flowing ceaselessly from her eyes. "I have to go, Mother," I said as I hastened toward the east. As I was going, I looked back at her again and again. She was there waving her hand against the backdrop of the rising sun.

When I came to the railroad station, the waiting room was almost completely empty. I was not sure what was happening there, for it was usually filled with passengers in the early morning. Nevertheless, I decided to buy my ticket at the ticket counter. A man wearing a dark gray uniform approached me with a serious facial expression. "I have reserved a ticket to Unggi," I said, which was the city from which to make connections to Siberia. He said, "All reservations have been canceled by order of the Central Government." "Why?" I asked him. "We are at war with South Korea," he replied. He then continued, "The South

Koreans attacked us early this morning. You had better go home and stay there. No more travel for some time." When I heard it, I was severely shocked and lost any desire to go to Russia.

As I was returning to my mother, I thought of my older brother, who had joined the South Korean army. The war between the South and North Koreans seemed almost impossible. When I came to the place where my mother had bidden me the last farewell, I felt so guilty that I could not raise my head. A strong sense of shame came over me, because I had failed to do what I wanted. I stood there for some time, hesitating to move. Then I lifted up my eyes and saw my mother working in the corn field on the terrace of South Mountain. The corn was about half grown, for it was late June. When I saw her working so hard under the hot sun, I was not only painfully shamed, but also felt sorry for my mother. Nonetheless, I found the courage to approach her. In the back of my mind I rationalized my returning home on the basis of having an urgent message to convey to her. Therefore, I shouted: "We are at war with South Korea! We are at war with South Korea!" As soon as she heard my voice, she ran to me all the way from the corn field and embraced me tightly, saying, "You have returned home! You have returned home for good." I nodded my head and said, "It is the war, the war between the North and South Koreans." My mother did not care what I was saying. All she wanted was me, not what I had to say. With a hoe in one hand and my hand in the other, my mother walked peacefully and joyously with me to our home. This experience of returning home with my mother was the greatest joy that I have ever had in my life.

About five years after this experience, I became a Christian and chanced to read the story of the prodigal son in Luke. Then I knew that I was a prodigal son. It was not my father but my mother against whom my disobedience was directed. The experience of having to return home plunged me into strong feelings of guilt and shame. I knew that I had committed a sin against her; but she was concerned about me, not about my sin or guilt. In the Bible I saw a similar attitude in the father, who paid little attention to what his son said, but was instead overwhelmed with joy over the return of his son. The father said nothing about the forgiveness of sins when his son said: "Father, I have sinned against God and against you. I am no longer fit to be called your son." The father completely ignored what the son said. His forgiveness was implicit in his action. What the father did was to ask his servants to bring out the best robe and shoes and to roast the fatted calf for celebration. His concern was for the son himself. "For this son of mine was dead, but now he is alive," he jubilated; "he was lost, but now he has been found." My mother felt exactly the same way when I tried to tell her about the war between the North and South Koreans. She paid no attention to what I said but only to what I was. Her joy at having me back at home outweighed all other concerns. And her action in walking me home hand in hand bore her tacit forgiveness. Thus, the story of the prodigal son in the Bible is the story of my own experience. That is why I am the prodigal son.

After reading the Bible story and reflecting upon my own experience, I began to think of the prodigal son from two different perspectives: first from the perspective of the son and then from that of the father. From the perspective of the son it did not seem to be a sin worthy of guilt to leave home against the will of the father. When the son failed to accomplish what he set out to do, however, he began to realize his sin against his father. I felt the same. I had no sense of guilt or shame at all when I left my mother against her will. But when, owing to circumstances beyond my control, I had to come back, then I felt guilty. If I had succeeded in going to Russia as the prodigal son succeeded at becoming self-sufficient, I would never have felt guilty as I did. It seems in general, then, that we become aware or conscious of our sin mainly when we fail in life. Nevertheless, our fathers or mothers do not judge us in terms of success or failure; they just accept us as their children. Our parents' concern is either to have us or not to have us. It is for them an existential question, which is far more fundamental than the functional question with which the son was preoccupied. Like parents' concern for their children, God's concern for us is far more fundamental than our concern for God or even for ourselves. God is concerned with us in terms of his love for our whole being, while we are concerned with God and with ourselves in terms of gain or loss, success or failure.

From my experience of becoming the prodigal son, I have learned the value of patience and long-suffering, which are destined to triumph in the end. Our arrogance and pride are buried only when we become desperate. If we regard ourselves as sojourners upon the earth like the prodigal son, our homecoming is "joy before the angels of God" (Luke 15:10), irrespective of our failure or success in this world. The unconditional love of our God is, then, the only hope of universal salvation. Let us rejoice for the assurance of his loving presence in our lives. Amen.

10

Do Not Worry About Tomorrow

Therefore do not be anxious about tomorrow, for tomorrow will be anxious for itself. Let the day's own trouble be sufficient for the day."

(Matthew 6:34)

We often think that Jesus was only interested in human relationships and social affairs, but he was interested in natural phenomena as well. The parables of the sower, the mustard seed, the vineyard, and the fig tree are good examples of his use of natural objects as a means of illustrating his message. Among his many other parables, those about birds and flowers seem to occupy an important place in Jesus' use of natural phenomena.

Let us look at the text, especially at the portion where Jesus mentions the birds and flowers. He said, "Look at the birds of the air. . . . Consider the lilies of the field, how they grow" (Matthew 6:26-28). Jesus wants us to learn something from these natural objects by observing them carefully. Jesus stresses close observation, using such words as "look at," "consider," or "how they grow." This seems to imply that we can learn through the careful observation of nature. Scientific knowledge, for example, comes from a careful observation of natural phenomena. Observation became important in the development of science and technology. Nowadays, an electron microscope is used to observe the minuscule world of microbiology for the greater understanding of natural phenomena. Most of our knowledge comes from the careful observation of nature.

When Jesus said "look at" or "consider," he was interested in the spiritual and moral lessons to be gained through our observation. Observing the birds in the air and the flowers in the field, we learn how they live. They become a metaphor of our own living. They are not anxious, nor do they worry about tomorrow. They eat what is available and are satisfied. Most of them do not even store food for the winter season. They give no thought to tomorrow. They take things as they come. The flowers do not worry about what is going to happen to them. The frost may come tomorrow, or someone may come to take away the flower; yet, the flowers do not worry. Their life is then that of faith, the life of trust; for they do not worry about the future. They trust that tomorrow will take care of itself. This kind of trust is also needed by us if we are to live each day as it comes.

The best way to learn from the birds and flowers is to participate in their lives. Careful observation here means more than objective observation; it also means that we should identify ourselves with them. In other words, we must put ourselves in the place of the birds and flowers and empathize with them if we are to learn something from them. We cannot understand them without becoming a part of them. Therefore, our moral and spiritual learning from natural objects is possible only through our active participation in their lives.

It is difficult for people in the Western tradition to identify with natural objects, such as birds and flowers, for natural objects have been regarded as inferior. However, in the Eastern tradition one feels a strong affinity with nature. Man and nature are so inseparably related and united that one can easily identify oneself with other natural objects. Since people are none other than a part of nature, they can empathize with natural objects. A poignant example is found in the writing of a certain primary school student, who won first place in a national writing contest in South Korea. It deals with her experience of being the *stairs* in the school building. She identified herself as the stairs when she wrote the piece, and by thus becoming one with the stairs she could experience the pain and patience of the stairs.

We are also asked to learn from the birds and flowers by becoming one with them. We cannot understand how the birds and flowers feel unless we become a part of them. Therefore, as the little primary school girl did with the stairs, we also need to have the experience of being birds and flowers by our empathic participation. When Jesus said "look at" or "consider" something, he meant for us to view it not through detachment or objective observation but through participation or empathic observation. Through participatory observation we can learn life's wisdom from the birds and flowers. One of the insights we can learn from them is to trust, to trust that God will take care of us. Therefore, we do not have to worry about tomorrow.

The life of Jesus was similar to that of the birds and flowers. Jesus did not have his own home to stay in or bins in which to store food for the next day. He did not accumulate any property or possess any assets to secure his future. He lived one day at a time. He lived the day as it came, without worrying about tomorrow. He lived like the birds and flowers, for he was completely depending on God.

Our trust in God makes us content with the now, the present situation. The life of today is sufficient. Our life should be an expression of gratitude for what we have been, rather than the selfish expectation of what we would like to have. It is our anticipation and selfish desire that make us anxious about tomorrow. If we do not have any anticipation of outcomes, we do not have to worry about tomorrow. Moreover, if we do not have the selfish desire to know of our predicament ahead of time, we do not have to worry about tomorrow either. When we are preoccupied with the success or failure, gain or loss, and pleasure or pain of the future, we will worry about the outcome. Moreover, we will not have to worry about things which, in fact, are beyond our control.

The primary cause of worrying about tomorrow is our anticipation of things in process. During the Korean War, I had to go to the old high school building, which was used as a center for drafting young people into the army. I took the physical examination there, like the rest of the young people, after which I was asked to answer a few questions dealing with the doctrinal aspects of Communism in North Korea, where I lived. I answered all of the questions satisfactorily, except for one question that dealt with my elder brother. The officer asked me about the situation of my elder brother. I told him that he had gone to South Korea and joined the South Korean Army. Hearing it, he asked, "Are you willing to kill him if you see him on the battlefield?" I could not do that, so I kept silent. The officer thus concluded that I was not ready to join the North Korean Army. He put me in a room where a couple dozen young people were sitting. A few minutes later an intelligence officer came into the room, lined us up, and started to interrogate us brutally. The interrogation began from the right. He began to beat the youths with a dark leather strap. I saw the blood coming out of the back of the first youth and shedding on the wooden floor. The young man was beaten so ruthlessly that he was half dead. After the first one was beaten up, then the second man was also interrogated in the same way. As I was watching them suffering and was anticipating that soon I would be next, my entire body was shaking violently with fear and worries about my own suffering to come. It was almost unbearable to anticipate the outcome of my own torment. My anticipation, in fact, caused me more pain than the actual torment I would receive. My selfishness, my desire to avoid my own suffering, and the inevitable anticipation of my own predicament heightened my pain. If I had been genuinely concerned about those who had been tortured, I would not have worried about my own suffering. If I had not been a selfish person, I could have taken their suffering to myself, rather than worrying about my own suffering. It was my selfishness that made me anxious about my own suffering.

If we were truly concerned with those who are starving and without shelter in our time, we would be grateful for our own lot. Our proper attitude toward God is only that of thanksgiving. We should take the day or the moment as it comes. We must be content with what we are. We must live this moment as fully as we can without regrets. If tomorrow comes, we will take it as God's gift and rejoice in it. Do not worry about tomorrow. Let tomorrow take care of itself. Living this day without being anxious about tomorrow is the secret of a happy life. Let us live now fully and trust in God, who gives us each morning the grace to live another day. Amen.

11

The Vine and the Branches

*I am the vine, you are the branches.
He who abides in me, and I in him, he it is that bears much fruit, for
apart from me you can do nothing."*

(John 15:5)

A few years ago I visited Madeira, a beautiful island off
Portugal, where one of the world's finest wines is produced. I
saw many vineyards on steep hillsides there. While looking at
them as our bus passed by, I recalled what Jesus said to his
disciples: "I am the vine, you are the branches." Jesus'
teaching reflected the circumstances of his own day in Israel.
He no doubt saw many vineyards when he walked along the
path, as I did in Madeira.

If you have never seen a vineyard, you can simply imagine a
complete grapevine, consisting of a short stem and many
branches. The vine or stem symbolizes Christ, and the
branches the Christians or congregations of them. Thus, the
grapevine can stand as a symbol of the church, where the
people of God are joined together with Christ. As a member
of the church, I want to think of myself as a branch of the
grapevine.

The branch is not self-sufficient, for it is totally dependent
on the vine. The branch exists because of the vine, even

though the vine may exist by itself without the branch. As a branch of the grapevine, I cannot claim my own autonomy. If I do not abide in him (Christ), as a branch of the vine, I become like a withered stick to be thrown into the fire and burned. I have life because I am connected to him, just as a branch lives because it is connected to the vine.

Nevertheless, I would like to be self-sufficient. I want to be independent. I act as if I am of my own self. I think as if I am not bound to Christ. When I fail in business or in study, I take it as a matter of my own responsibility. When I succeed in life, I think that it was made possible by my own ability and take the credit to myself. Yet as a branch, I should by rights give the credit to the vine from which I draw my strength and vitality. When the vine is weak, the branch partakes of its weakness; when the vine is destroyed, the branch is destroyed along with it.

It was in the year 1945, the year when Japan surrendered to America in the Second World War, that most Koreans were left without food. Almost all crops that the Koreans produced had been sent to Japan to feed the soldiers. At that time I was living on a small farm. In the early spring of that year I, as a young boy, had to go into the mountains to peel off the bark from the pine trees. Many people in the farm town did the same thing. The bark was brought home and boiled to make soup for drinking. Many people died of starvation, but the pine bark kept us alive through this critical time. I noticed, however, that the pine trees died because their trunks were naked. A tree without the protection of the outer layers of its trunk cannot survive, even though it might survive without its branches. Likewise, when Christ is no longer with us, we cannot live as Christians.

Just as the vine or stem is more important than the branches, Christ is prior to the Christians. When the grapevine lacks nourishment, it sacrifices its branches before it sacrifices the vine. Likewise, Christ takes priority in our lives. Jesus said, "If anyone comes after me, let him deny himself and take up his cross and follow me. Whoever gains his life will lose it, and whoever loses his life for my sake will find it." By losing our lives for the sake of Christ—that is, by losing the branches for the sake of the vine—we can save our lives. When the time comes for us to decide either for Christ or for ourselves, we must be like the branches bound to the vine; we must choose Christ before ourselves.

I had a friend who became a Christian during the Korean War. He volunteered as a YMCA worker and went to North Korea during the time when the UN forces had pushed the Communist armies all the way to the north of Pyongyang, the capital of North Korea. He wanted to become a missionary to the North Koreans, who had lost their faith owing to the oppressive policy of the Communist government with respect to religious liberty. While he was deeply involved in his mission work, the UN forces retreated suddenly from North Korea and left him behind. Eventually the Communists returned to Pyongyang and captured him. When he was asked to explain his status, he honestly told the Communist soldiers that he had come to spread the gospel to his people in Pyongyang. Hearing this, the soldiers blindfolded him for execution. But before they executed him, they asked him to say his last words. Instead of saying a word, he asked to sing his favorite hymn: "Just As I Am." He sang it so beautifully that it inspired the soldiers. These men, who had never been Christians before and were strongly against the Christians, were moved by his singing and released him. Although he was ready and willing to give up his life rather than betray his commitment to Christ, he was saved from having to do so. In a mysterious way, God saved his life. Jesus' word that anyone "who loses his life for my sake will find it" (Matthew 10:3a) became literally true for him.

In the early days, missionaries and Christian pioneers had to face the inevitable choice of siding with Christ, the vine, or with their own lives, the branches. When they took the side of the vine, or Christ, they often became martyrs. One of the most interesting books to be published in recent times is *Silence,* by the Japanese author Endo. In this book he narrates the apostasy of Portuguese missionaries in the sixteenth century in Japan. In those days the Japanese government oppressed the missionary movement, using all forms of inhumane treatment and torture. New converts to Christianity were often hung on a cross on the seashore, where the tide would come up and cover them to their chins so that they died gradually. They were also dipped in boiling water to test their loyalty to Christ. In order to avoid this unbearable torture, a certain Portuguese missionary renounced his faith in Christ and tramped upon a picture of Mary as the sign of his apostasy. His life was saved because of his apostasy, but he was forced to collaborate with the Japanese government to destroy Christianity. Nevertheless, Christianity survived in Japan, while the apostate destroyed himself in the end. As Jesus said, "He who finds his life will lose it." The branch cannot save its own life without the vine. It is the vine that takes priority over the branch.

Christ and Christians are united, just as the vine and branches are in unity. Jesus said: "Abide in me, and I in you. As the branch cannot bear fruit by itself, unless it abides in the vine, neither can you, unless you abide in me" (John 15:4). The vine and branches are so organically united that they are one. The branches are none other than extensions of the vine, just as the vine is the origin of the branches. This kind of organic unity between Christ and his people is possible because of love, which is the power that unites the separated. "As the Father has loved me, so have I loved you; abide in my love. If you keep my commandments, you will abide in my love, just as I have kept my Father's commandments and abide in his love" (John 15:9, 10). It is love that unites them into one.

During the Korean War, in 1950, I was hiding underground for three months, in order to avoid being drafted into the Red Army. My mother brought me food late in the evenings. One evening she came in and sat right next to me. Seeing that she was trembling with fear, I knew that something was wrong.

"Please tell me. What is it?" I asked impatiently.

She held me tightly and then put her mouth to my ear. Her entire body was shaking. Then she said: "Yesterday, your friend, so-and-so, who was hiding in a cave as you have been, was discovered by the police. This afternoon he was executed in front of the townspeople. Everyone saw it. His parents were so violently tortured by the whip in front of the townspeople that they became unconscious and then died. It was so terrible that I could not look at them any longer. They were whipped and whipped until they died, because they were responsible for hiding their son underground."

When I heard this, I was ready to run away. I said, "Let me run away from here as far as I can. Or let me volunteer to go to the Army tomorrow, so that you don't have to be whipped to death."

My mother held me so tightly that I could not move. Her voice was urgent. "No. Your life is also our life. If we die, we all die together."

I saw her tears shining in the darkness like diamonds. It was an expression of unity in love. I experienced a oneness with my mother in that moment. Just as the vine extends to its branches, so also did my mother's whole self extend to me. It was her love that united us.

In God's love we become extensions of Christ, just as the branches are extensions of the vine. The fruit is the by-product of this unity of love. When we are united with Christ, like the branches with the vine, we become creative. The fruit is the outward manifestation of our inner unity with

Christ. By the fruit we prove ourselves to be disciples of Christ. The fruit of love is joy.

"I am the vine, you are the branches." The vine is Christ, and the branches are his people. Thus, the grapevine is the symbol of our church, where the people are united with Christ. Although there are many branches, they do not all bear fruit, for they are not all completely united with the vine. Some of them are withered. They need to be pruned out, for they are Christians by name only. It is only those branches that are united with the vine that can bear the fruit of love, which is joy. In this symbolic unity between the vine and its branches, Jesus fulfills his wish "that my joy may be in you, and that your joy may be full" (John 15:11). Amen.

12

The Lord's Supper

He ordered the crowd to sit down on the ground. Then he took the seven loaves, gave thanks to God, broke them, and gave them to his disciples to distribute to the crowd; and the disciples did so. They also had a few small fish. Jesus gave thanks for these and told the disciples to distribute them too. Everybody ate and had enough—there were about four thousand people. Then the disciples took up seven baskets full of pieces left over. Jesus sent the people away.

(Mark 8:6-9 GNB)

Although the passage found in our text is often understood as describing a miracle, I would like to regard it as a prototype of the communion service or Lord's Supper. If we consider it as a form of communion, there were more than four thousand people who participated in the service.

From the passage we notice that a great crowd of people followed after Jesus for three days. This following seems to indicate that these people were so deeply immersed in the ministry of Jesus that they did not even take time to eat their meals. I would like to compare this with my own experience of participating in one of the mass evangelical meetings in Seoul, Korea, before I came to this country about thirty years ago. The meeting in which I took part was a retreat attended by more than five thousand people, all of whom came to receive spiritual blessings. I too, stayed there for three days without food. Once I had joined the meeting, I had no desire to leave it for a meal. I continued there with them singing and praying together. It was in part a fast as well as a spiritual experience. I did not know that I was hungry for three days even though I did not eat a meal (though I had a few drinks of water from the public well). When the service was over, I was almost completely exhausted and nearly fainted. However, the evangelist did not stay to care for our health; he left by himself before the group was dispersed.

Jesus, however, was different from that evangelist. According to our text, Jesus was concerned not only with our spiritual life but also with our physical welfare. He said, "I have compassion on the crowd, because they have been with me now three days, and have nothing to eat; and if I send them away hungry to their homes, they will faint on the way, and some of them have come a long way" (Mark 8:2, 3). Jesus here manifests his compassion, being concerned with the whole person. The evangelist who left by himself without caring for the people who had fasted for three days was not only insensitive to their total needs but did not have compassion on them. Jesus' concern for the crowd, and especially for those who were hungry, demonstrated his love for the needy people.

If we take this passage as a form of communion service, we begin to realize that the communion is not a simple ritual reenactment but an actual feeding of hungry people. In other words, the Lord's Supper is not a pure spiritual rite but an actual experience of partaking of food together with the poor and hungry. Those who partake of the communion service not only remember those who are hungry in the world but also actually experience the presence of Jesus with the hungry people. The bread of which we partake at communion is more than just a symbol. It is the real bread that Jesus served to the four thousand people who followed him. Therefore, when we take communion, we remember not only the death and resurrection of Christ but also those who are hungry in the world.

The communion service is also that of our thankfulness to God. However insignificant it might be, we should express our thanks to God. We learn from the passage in Mark 8 that there were only a few pieces of bread, but that Jesus gave thanks before he broke them. The few loaves in the presence of four thousand people was almost nothing, and worthless. Yet, he gave thanks for it. It shows how thankful a person Jesus was; he did not take anything for granted.

In our time we have the tendency to take everything for granted. We have lost our sense of gratitude and do not know how to appreciate the things we have in our lives. We usually have plenty to eat; most of us never go to bed with hungry stomachs. To those who are hungry, however, a single piece of bread is precious. If we have not eaten for three days, one piece of bread means a great deal. Everything that we eat is tasty if we are hungry. Therefore, we can express our genuine thanks for the food when we are truly hungry and in need.

I remember the time when I worked at Pusan Harbor during the Korean War in 1950. I was a refugee from North Korea and had found a job in the harbor unloading U.S. Army rations from the ship. One day I was waiting for the ship to arrive at the harbor. At that time I was very hungry, for I had not had a decent meal for a couple of days. As soon as the ship arrived, I saw an American soldier who threw a piece of a sandwich at me. I grabbed it as it came down and started to eat it as fast as I could. It was so tasty that I could hardly express it in words. At that time I did not know what kind of sandwich it was. However, after I came to America, I found out that it was a ham sandwich. I have eaten many ham sandwiches since coming to this country, but I have never enjoyed again the same taste that I found in the sandwich at

Pusan Harbor. The sandwich was so delicious because I was very hungry at that time. Since coming to this country, I have found ham sandwiches so readily available that I now take them for granted and forget to give thanks. Our genuine thanks and appreciation are expressed when we are truly in need.

As we come to take the communion service, we must come to the table as if we were truly hungry. We should approach it as though we were the four thousand people who had not had any food for three days. Unless we approach the Lord's Supper with hunger, we cannot appreciate it. Unless we are hungry, we cannot give thanks to God for the food we eat. We must come to the table with spiritual hunger as well. Unless we come with a thirst and a hunger for righteousness and love, we will never find the presence of Christ at the table.

The fellowship of those who come together is enhanced by eating meals together. An unusually close fellowship develops from the sharing of food. One of the best ways to get to know people is to invite them to a meal. By eating together we come to know one another more intimately than before. According to Korean custom, family members are known as those who eat the same food. In particular, the family is known as *Sipku*, which simply means the group of those who eat together. By eating together we become members of a family. In communion service we eat the meal with the Risen Christ. By doing so we become members of the family of Christ. Through the sharing of bread and drink with Christ, we are joined together in turn as members of the household of God. Regardless of race, nationality, or creed, anyone who comes to participate in the Lord's Supper becomes our brother or sister in the family of God. This is the true meaning of partaking of the bread with wine at the communion service.

Although the actual presence of Christ at the table of our communion service is undeniable, this presence is spiritual. In other words, the physical and actual presence of Christ at the original table became the prototype of today's communion service. The Passover meal with Jesus in the upper room is enacted again and again at our communion services. In this respect the communion service in which we participate can also be understood as a commemorative meal. It is a meal for the commemoration of Jesus and his death.

In Korea there is a commemorative service and meal for the departed at least once a year. The service is usually held in the fall when the new crops have been harvested. I remember the day when all of our family got together to visit the ancestral tombs. We took many different kinds of food made from the new crops. We placed the food and drink before the ancestral tomb and performed a certain Confucian rite. My father used to read a passage from the writings of a Confucian classic before we shared the meal together in front of the grave. During the meal, my father used to tell us the story of our dead ancestors, thus perpetuating their memory. If my father had been a Christian at that time, he would no doubt have read the Christian liturgy at the commemorative service of our dead ancestors. However, what impressed me most in the service was the stories about the ancestors.

Our communion service is also a commemorative service for the death of Christ. Therefore, during the service we must remember the stories of the life of Christ. It is a time to recall the life and death of Christ for the salvation of our souls. Especially, we must remember how much he suffered on the cross before his death and his departure from the world. As we come to the table of the Lord's Supper, we must spend enough time there to meditate upon the events in the life of Christ.

However, the communion service that we celebrate is more than a memorial service for the departed Christ; it is also a service of real communion with the living Christ, for Christ has risen from the dead. Jesus Christ, who served the meals to the four thousand people on the hill by the Sea of Galilee, is present in our service. He is with us as the cosmic Christ, whose presence is everywhere. He is not only present among us in spirit but actually gives us of himself in the form of bread and wine. He is the one who also serves us, as he served the four thousand. In a way we join them and become part of their company, too, as we participate in the communion service. The people in the past are brought up into the present and become part of our fellowship. Moreover, the people around the world are joined together with us in the communion service, for the same Christ is present everywhere. In this service the people before us and after us are joined together and become the one household of God. This, then, is the true communion of the living and of the saints in Christ.

The bread we partake of at the service of communion is not only the symbol of Christ's body but also the real bread that Jesus fed the hungry people who followed him. It is the real bread that nourishes the millions of hungry and starving people around the world. Christ himself represented this bread for the world. By this bread our whole selves are nourished. Also the partakers of this bread and wine are brought together as members of Christ's family. We rejoice, therefore, for the opportunity to partake of the communion service. Let us partake of it with thanksgiving. Let us come to it with hunger and thirst for new life in Christ. May we then truly experience the indwelling Christ in our hearts as we partake of the bread and wine at the Lord's table. Amen.

13

The New Family in Christ

Do not think that I have come to bring peace on earth; I have not come to bring peace, but a sword. For I have come to set a man against his father, and a daughter against her mother, and a daughter-in-law against her mother-in-law; and a man's foes will be those of his own household. He who loves father or mother more than me is not worthy of me; and he who loves son or daughter more than me is not worthy of me; and he who does not take his cross and follow me is not worthy of me. He who finds his life will lose it, and he who loses his life for my sake will find it."

(Matthew 10:34-39)

This is the most difficult teaching of Jesus that I have ever confronted in my study of the New Testament. Why did Jesus say that he came to bring a sword rather than peace? Do we not call him the Prince of Peace? Did he not say that the peacemakers receive God's blessings? Did he not say that we must go to our brothers for reconciliation before we ask God's forgiveness? How could he then say that he came to destroy the peace and disrupt our family life? Why did he want to break up our family? Is not the family a divine institution? There are countless questions that the text presents to us. How can we deal with this text in light of the other teachings of Jesus? Can we simply dismiss it as if it were irrelevant to the central teachings of Jesus? No. I think this text is very important for anyone aspiring to understand the meaning of discipleship. Therefore, I would like to take it seriously and try to understand the spirit of the text in terms of my own experience in the past.

First of all, the text definitely declares that our family relationship may be destroyed because of Christ. One's commitment to Christ and one's discipleship sets one apart from one's family. The very destruction of the family seems to be implicit in the text. In other words, the family based on flesh and blood has to be destroyed through the coming of Christ, so that a new relationship can develop in the spirit. The old order needs to be renewed. However, the renewal of the old presupposes the destruction of the old.

Let me illustrate this principle in terms of my own experience. I came to the United States in the early 1950s to study chemistry. When I came to my senior year I applied for graduate study in chemistry. Then a month later I returned to my major adviser, who was also the academic dean in a small college in Ohio, and told him that I had changed my mind. I said, "I have decided to go to a seminary to become a minister." The dean was dumbfounded when he heard it. "Are you sure?" he said. He thought I was joking. I told him that I was serious, that I had received the call to become a minister. Knowing that he could not persuade me to pursue further my study in chemistry, he decided to support my plan to enter a theological seminary. A few weeks later I was invited to attend a seminar for pre-theological students on the Oberlin College campus, where I had the opportunity to talk to counselors about my decision to go to a seminary. All of those to whom I talked strongly discouraged me. They wanted me to continue my studies in chemistry. Nevertheless, I decided to apply for admission to Garrett Theological Seminary. Luckily for me, the seminary accepted my application.

Meanwhile, I wrote letters to my father in Korea and told him of my decision to enroll in a theological seminary in order to become a Christian minister. My father wrote me again and again that I should continue my studies in chemistry. In one letter he said, "If you decide to go to a seminary by disobeying my wish, I will have to disown you." I asked for his understanding and begged him to forgive my disobedience. When I finally made up my mind to go to the seminary, he wrote me a last letter and said, "You are no longer my son. You are free to do whatever you want to do. You don't have a father, and I don't have a son anymore." At the end of the letter he said, "It is still not too late for you to change your mind." When I received this letter, my heart was torn and I cried bitterly. I did not know what to do. As an Oriental I had to maintain the virtue of filial piety, which is regarded as the cornerstone of all other virtues. In the Oriental tradition the father has absolute authority over his son. It is, therefore, almost impossible to go against the demand of the father. I knew that very well when I received his letter. I had to obey my father, but at the same time I had to obey the call of God to the ministry, too. Torn between the two conflicting demands, I did not know what to do. I struggled for several days and nights, praying and searching my heart for a solution. At the end I decided to give my loyalty to God and to his call to the ministry. It was the most painful decision I have ever made in my life. I had to go against my father. The day when I wrote him my final decision to go to the seminary, my relation with my father was over. My father did not write to me anymore; I lost my father.

About a month after arriving at Garrett Theological Seminary, I received a letter from my elder brother. I was so excited at first to receive a letter from home, for I had not heard from home for many months. However, when I opened the letter and read it, I was greatly saddened. He said: "It is not too late for you to change your mind. This will be the last

letter from me, too, if you don't get away from the seminary."
Again I felt a great pain in my heart. I became lonely, for
everyone seemed to go against me. I wanted to belong to my
family. Yet I would have to give up my ministry if I wanted to
be a part of them.

Holding the letter in my hand, I went to a small chapel. It
was dark inside, and no one was there. I prayed and prayed
that God would give me an answer. I am not sure what I said
to God or how I said it. But the next thing I knew, I had
awakened on my bed in the dormitory. My roommate and his
friend came to me and said: "We saw you in the chapel. We
didn't know what to do. You were lying on the floor and were
unconscious. So we brought you to your room." I looked at
my watch; it was eleven o'clock. I felt that I had become a
different person. I did not have to worry anymore about my
family in Korea. I was almost completely relieved from my tie
with my family. I felt that I had found a new family in Christ.
Christ then became my brother and God my father.

For three years I did not receive a single letter from my
father or my brother. I knew that I had been disowned by
them. When Christ came into my life, my family life was
almost destroyed; my alienation from my family was nearly
total. Christ brought a sword to my family, which divided us,
myself and my father. I was completely cut off from my family
in Korea because of my commitment to become a disciple of
Christ.

However, the division due to my commitment to Christ
was a necessary prerequisite for the new relationship. The
old relationship that existed in my family was gone because of
Christ, but a new relationship was born out of the destruction
of the old relationship. A few months before my graduation
from the seminary, I received a letter from my father, the first
since I entered the seminary. It was a letter of reconciliation.
God had worked in him to reconcile our broken relationship,
for my father had become a Christian, and my relationship

with him was restored in Christ. In this respect, the new relationship was based upon Christ, while the old had been without him. Thus, out of the destruction of the old relationship, the new relationship in Christ was born. God's ultimate aim is not destruction but the renewal of the old for our salvation.

From my own experience, it is clear that the passage we are dealing with is relevant to those families who are non-Christian; the text is directed to unbelieving families. When one of the members believes in Christ, the family breaks down.

I have also witnessed another family broken because of Christ. One of my friends went to the same tent meeting where I was converted to Christianity. His family, knowing that he had become a Christian, was unhappy, for it was a family of Confucian background. One day he was forced to go to the ancestral temple to worship his ancestors. He felt, however, that he could not participate in the ancestor worship because of his commitment to Christ; he viewed such worship as a form of idolatry. In order to avoid the ancestor worship, he ran away from home. His family was disrupted because of his commitment to Christ. In a way, Christ came to his family to create conflict, not peace. I do not know whether a reconciliation between him and his family has ever taken place, but his experience illustrates the text very well. What Jesus said in the Gospel seems to be relevant to unbelieving families. We know that most of the people living at the time of Jesus were not believers in Christ. Therefore, what is said makes sense. For those who are members of a Christian family, on the other hand, this passage does not make sense. It is to be understood only in the context of those who are living in a civilization that is alien to or against Christianity.

However, the text is directed to believers as well. For those who have already become a part of Christianity, Jesus demands their absolute obedience to him. When we find ourselves in a conflict between our own family members and Christ, we must choose Christ before our family. Christ comes before anyone else; he demands our absolute obedience. Anyone who loves his father or mother more than he loves Christ is not worthy of becoming a disciple of Christ. Our love of Christ must transcend all other loves. We must be ready to follow Christ at any time and at any cost. When we make our unfailing commitment to Christ, we begin to realize that the new relationship evolves out of the old one. In this new relationship, Christ becomes the cornerstone and foundation of our relationship with others; that is, we became a new family in Christ. The spiritual relationship coming from Christ becomes the inner strength of our human relationships. In this respect, anyone who "loses his life for my sake will find it." Losing our old relationship, we find a new relationship that is much better than the old. Let us lose ourselves for the sake of Christ, so that we may find ourselves anew in Christ. Amen.

14

Loneliness

The hour is coming, indeed it has come, when you will be scattered, every man to his home, and will leave me alone; yet I am not alone, for the Father is with me."
(John 16:32)

The autumn season arouses in me a sense of loneliness. The richness of the green leaves and the vitality of the plants are gone in the fall; the beautiful foliage does not stay very long. The leaves begin to fall, and the trees start to bare themselves as the cold northern wind blows upon them. The summer months are characterized by the growth and expansion of all things, but the fall months are marked by the decay and cessation of all things. Fall is a time of silence and contemplation. It is also the time of the ripening of fruits and crops and then of the harvest. The ripened fruits begin to separate themselves from the trees and fall to the ground. This separation makes them lonely. The trees that drop their fruits are also lonely.

Our families are somewhat similar to the changing seasons. When we are children, we are like the tiny green fruits that are tightly connected to the trees. Children and parents are tightly connected together, so that neither is lonely as long as they are together. The period of childhood can be compared to the spring season. In the spring the fruits are born from the flowers. As the fruits grow and expand in the summer, so the children grow to become youths. The period of youth can be compared to the summer season. Then when the children are fully grown up, they start to leave home. Thus, the maturity of our children can be compared to the fall season. When the children depart from home they leave their parents alone. This separation makes both the grown-up children and the parents lonely. Loneliness, then, is an inherent part of the process of growth and maturation.

Our society today, as it becomes mature, is also characterized by the sense of loneliness. In earlier days we had to work hard to develop the social and economic conditions in which we live. This was a period of toil, with its physical pain and suffering. Today American society seems to have reached the season of autumn. Our economic growth has slowed down, and our political power in the world has begun to diminish. This signifies the beginning of the fall season. It has been primarily the powers of scientific technology that have eliminated our physical suffering and pain and ushered our society into the process of maturation. Scientific technology is also responsible for the creation of a society in which the problems of loneliness and alienation, rather than those of physical pain and suffering, have become real issues. When physical problems are under control, it is then that psychological problems come to the fore in human life. And basic to all of the psychological problems in our lives is the sense of loneliness.

Our lives are characterized by loneliness because we are like the ripened fruits falling from the tree. When I drive my car, for example, to go to the school or to the store, I have thereby shielded myself from others. By cooping myself up in the car, I have alienated myself from them. I am separated when I am alone. This separation makes me like a fruit fallen to the ground. I often wonder whether it would be better if we did not have our cars to drive to work or shopping. If everyone would walk to school or to the store, people could greet one another and lessen the sense of loneliness. When I was in Tokyo some time ago, the busiest street, Ginja, was blocked off from automobile traffic, so that people could walk in the street. They seemed to enjoy being together in the open.

Our society has come to value individualism and privacy more as it has become more efficient and mature. But privacy and individualism presuppose independence and separation, which are the cause of loneliness. If loneliness, however, is a by-product of maturity and independence, it should not be regarded as purely negative. Loneliness can, in fact, be more positive than negative in its impact upon us. To be sure, loneliness can be destructive when it is taken negatively, but it can also be constructive when it is taken positively. Let us look, then, at the positive value of loneliness from a Christian perspective.

If we look at the life of Jesus, we see that it was a lonely one. He was born in the village of Bethlehem, which was not the hometown of his parents. He was born not only in an alien town but also of a mother who was not yet married. Jesus was doubtless ridiculed by his friends in the small and conservative town of Nazareth. Although we know little of his early life, we do know that at twelve years of age he was with the elders and learned men in the Temple discussing interpretations of the Scriptures. This seems to indicate that he felt closer to older people than to his own peers. Like many precocious children who lack friends of their own age, Jesus often found himself alone. Moreover, he felt the need to spend many years by himself in meditation and prayer. We know from the Scriptures that he spent forty days and forty nights in the wilderness right after his baptism by John the Baptist. Although a crowd of people followed him when he began his ministry, they did not understand him or share their feelings with him as a friend. Even his disciples failed to understand him. He did not have his own family; he did not have a home; he was alone much of the time. He could not rely on anyone. Even one of his own disciples betrayed him. Another of his most trusted disciples, Peter, also denied him three times. We remember Jesus' agony and loneliness in Gethsemane. When he was accused, no one sided with him or defended him. He was rejected and ridiculed by the Jewish leaders of the day. He had to carry the heavy cross alone. Those who had been faithful to him during his ministry became bystanders at his crucifixion; they were scattered all over when Jesus was nailed to the cross. Thus, Jesus said, "The hour is coming, indeed it has come, when you will be scattered, every man to his own home, and will leave me alone; yet I am not alone, for the Father is with me." Certainly, he was a lonely man as he walked this earth.

Jesus was a lonely man when we look at him from an earthly perspective. Nevertheless, he was not a lonely man in the ultimate sense; as he said, "Yet I am not alone, for the Father is with me." If loneliness is the feeling of being alone, he was not a lonely person because of his fellowship with his Father. Using an expression from Asian philosophy, we can say that the detachment of Jesus from the world was also his attachment to the spiritual world. As paradoxically stated by Buddhist or Taoist philosophers, detachment is also attachment. Jesus' detachment from the people expressed his loneliness, but his attachment to the Father implied togetherness. We can then say that Jesus' loneliness was also a togetherness, just as his detachment was also an attachment. Likewise, although Jesus had few friends, he became a friend to all. In a way, detachment was necessary in order for him to attach himself totally to the world. This is the kind of paradox through which we can learn to overcome our loneliness.

As Christians we are asked to follow the way of Christ. We are asked to bear the cross by ourselves without the assistance of others. To bear the cross alone means to stand alone through tribulation and oppression. As Christians we must not shun loneliness. For Christians loneliness is, in fact, an opportunity to be with Christ, just as it was for Jesus to be with his Father. In loneliness we can turn our thoughts inward. Our solitariness affords us the time to detach our thinking from the external things that detract our thoughts from God and from spiritual issues. It is our loneliness that yields us a profound sense of detachment from the world, which in turn is the means for a greater attachment to the world and its needs than ever before. Therefore, we should not be ashamed of being alone.

Somehow we come to be afraid of the loneliness in our lives. I see many people in the college cafeteria who go through the line and are then afraid to sit by themselves. They hate to sit alone because some people look down upon those who do not have others sitting with them; they are presumed to have no friends. They feel that they have to join others even if they do not know them. I have seen people who wanted to eat in the cafeteria, but who had to leave because they could not find anyone to eat with. Many of us are afraid of loneliness and try to avoid it at all costs. It is especially true of many teenagers that they feel compelled to do things they do not really want to do because of their fear of loneliness. Loneliness can be a powerful force if we yield to it. It can wield great power over us if we are ashamed of being alone.

We must learn to be proud of being alone. Through loneliness we learn to depend on God. Loneliness is a grace that keeps us aware of our insufficiency; it nourishes what Schleiermacher felt to be the essence of religion, our feeling of dependency. Loneliness is the feeling of the incompleteness of the self due to its separation from God. The cause of our separation from God is sin, and loneliness is the by-product of that separation. We know from the story of Adam and Eve in Genesis that their loneliness began only after their departure from the Garden of Eden. Before they left there, they were at one with God and in community with him; but then they sinned. It was that sin which separated us, and that separation makes us feel lonely. Therefore, the remedy for loneliness is to be found only in our relationship to God. By detaching ourselves from our selfishness, which separates us from the world, we can find real fellowship with God. This real fellowship alone is our Christian solution to the problem of loneliness. Jesus has demonstrated the way to solve this problem through his own detachment from the contaminated world and his attachment to the real and spiritual world.

Many years ago I was a foreign student in the theological seminary on the Northwestern University campus. When the Christmas season came, all the seminary students left the campus. By Christmas Eve, in fact, the huge dormitory was completely empty except for me; I was the only person who stayed. That evening I went outside and started to walk alone on the shore of Lake Michigan. White snow was falling on the sidewalk as I strolled along by myself, thinking of the Christmases I had had at home. I had no place to go, for no stores or restaurants were open. Therefore, I came back to my room on the third floor of the dormitory. When I opened the windows slightly because the room was so overheated, I heard the Christmas carol "Silent Night, Holy Night," which is one of my favorite songs. I almost completely lost myself and was caught up in rapture. I felt for some time that I had become the music itself. This was without a doubt the most beautiful and rewarding experience that I had ever had since coming to the seminary. I felt the spiritual presence at that moment, an experience made possible for me by the fact that I was alone—and lonely.

Loneliness provided for me an opportune time to be with God, who had always been close to me. In loneliness I became aware of the closeness of God. Since that experience I have come to place a positive value upon the sense of loneliness in my Christian life. Loneliness is a Christian virtue that transports our lives from the secular to the sacred level. Loneliness can break down the wall that separates us from God. It is, therefore, a means of grace and salvation. Amen.

15

Reconciliation

But I say to you that every one who is angry with his brother shall be liable to judgment; whoever insults his brother shall be liable to the council, and whoever says, 'You fool!' shall be liable to the hell of fire. So if you are offering your gift at the altar, and there remember that your brother has something against you, leave your gift there before the altar and go; first be reconciled to your brother, and then come and offer your gift."

(Matthew 5:22-24)

Paul describes the work of Christ as the ministry of reconciliation. This means that Christ was the peacemaker. He was the one whom Isaiah predicted as the Prince of Peace. He brought peace not only among people but also between God and humanity. To reconcile means to restore a broken relationship by removing some enmity that hinders a peaceful relationship. Christ came to the world to remove such a hindrance, to remove our sins, which prevent us from having communion with God. The removal of our sins is then the precondition of reconciliation. It is our sin that creates enmity between God and humanity and among people. Therefore, reconciliation is not possible without salvation. It is a mistake to separate salvation from reconciliation. They are one in two different manifestations.

Reconciliation can be conceived of as the final process of a twofold movement in salvation. When we think of salvation, we mean both the freedom from sin and the restoration of the original relationship with God. In other words, liberation from sin is not enough. Liberation "from" should lead to liberation "to." When we are liberated from sin, we are then brought back to the original relationship. Reconciliation is the restoring of the original relationship through liberation. It is none other than the final stage of salvation. Thus, salvation includes reconciliation, and at the same time reconciliation is a result of liberation.

If Christ came to reconcile the world to himself, his work of redemption is implicitly universal. Through his death and resurrection everyone is capable of salvation. God is working toward the salvation of all humanity, "not wishing that any should perish" (II Peter 3:9). Even though the actual work of universal salvation had already begun with the coming of Christ, the progress has been slow. The reason for this slowness can be a reflection of something in the process. We have a tendency to lay the emphasis upon the salvation of individual souls from sin. However, salvation is not complete unless the state of reconciliation has been reached. The process of reconciliation is slow, because it begins with human relationships. In other words, it begins with the most intimate relationship and expands to the universal relationship. This seems to belie the common assumption that our relationship with God is prior to our relationship with our own brothers and sisters. If we look at the text we have selected, however, it is quite clear that our relationships with one another come before our relation with God. We have to reconcile ourselves with our fellow human beings before we can ask for reconciliation with God. This is precisely why there is no instant reconciliation. There is neither automatic reconciliation nor instant salvation. The process of reconciliation begins with the intimate circle and expands to the community and finally to God.

This process of reconciliation from the intimate group to the broader community life is well known in the Asian way of life. It was Confucius who defined the five categories of human relationship. He said that every human being had to deal with five relationships: the relationship between parents and children, the relationship between husband and wife, the relationships among brothers or sisters, the relationship between the young and the old, and the relationship between the ruler and the ruled. Of these relationships the most important one—which becomes the foundation of all the others—is the relationship between parents and children. All other human relationships have to begin with this intimate relationship. Therefore, the central importance of the family in Confucianism is understandable. Unless the intimate relationship within the family is at peace and harmony, we cannot have peace with our neighbors either. Unless we can get along with our own people, we cannot hope for world peace. Likewise, we cannot expect peace with God unless we first find peace among ourselves.

Jesus, therefore, teaches us that we have to be reconciled with our brothers and sisters before we seek reconciliation with God. If we cannot settle those issues that are within our grasp among ourselves, we cannot expect to settle the issues that are beyond our reach. Peace begins at home and reaches out to the community and finally to the whole world. In other words, reconciliation begins with the intimate circle of human relationship, not with a God-human relationship. Unless I have made my peace with my fellow human beings, I cannot find peace with my God.

Many of you may have a unique story to share in connection with the problem of reconciliation with your fellow human beings. I have a story that I want to share with you, because it tells you how difficult it is to reconcile ourselves with someone we hate. The story begins with the carelessness of my college president, who had written a recommendation on my behalf to a theological seminary, where I was later enrolled. The president was unfamiliar with the system of theological education. Since he thought that I was a good student, he recommended me directly into a doctoral study program. The acting director of admissions at the seminary was also the professor of ethics. When he received this letter of recommendation, he was rather displeased. He wrote a nasty letter back to my college president explaining that no student, however brilliant, can directly enroll in the doctoral program; the student must first finish the program on the ministry. The president was unhappy and advised me to go to another seminary. Nevertheless, I did finally go to that seminary for study.

When I came to register for my freshman courses at the seminary, the acting director of admissions, who was also the professor of ethics, was there. He remembered me well. I asked him what courses I should take for the first semester. He said cynically, "Since you are such a bright student, you can take any courses you wish. Why do you have to worry!" After that, I knew that he did not like me, and I tried to avoid him as much as possible.

However, the ethics course that he taught was required for graduation; and by the end of my senior year, I could avoid him no longer. I found a seat in the rear of the classroom. I was a serious student, however, and decided to work unusually hard for this course to prove that I was a brilliant student. Most of the people who were taking this course were first- and second-year students; therefore, I thought that I could do better than most of them.

On the midterm examination, which was rather simple, I thought I did very well. When my roommate asked me about the midterm exam, I said, "I expect an A-grade; but I would be happy with a B." However, when I got the blue book back,

I found that my grade was F. It was unbelievable! There was no explanation of why I got an F-grade. I was angry at him and could hardly wait until the class was dismissed. I followed him to his office and demanded an explanation of why I received an F. His entire body was quivering; he could not control his emotions. He then said, "If I give you an F, that is it. If you have any complaint, go to the dean of students." I dashed upstairs and into the office of the dean of students. He heard my complaint and understood my feelings, but he could not do anything to change the grade. He said, "I cannot do a thing. It is up to the instructor. What he wants is to humiliate you." "I have known that since I came here," I said to myself.

When I took the final examination, it also turned out to be an F. Because I got an F, I was asked to take the course all over again. So I did so, and finally got a D—enough to pass the requirement. I became so hostile to the teacher that I could not even pass in front of his office. I avoided him, just as he avoided me. I came to realize, however, that I had to be reconciled with him before leaving the seminary. "I cannot be a minister of reconciliation, unless I can make reconciliation with my ethics teacher. I will have to give up my ministry if I cannot become reconciled with him." My mind was constantly preoccupied with the words of Jesus that we have read from Matthew 5, where one has to be reconciled with his neighbors before seeking reconciliation with his God. This was the most difficult task that I had ever confronted in my life. However, it was not possible to do it with my own power and courage. God gave me the grace to initiate my reconciliation with the teacher. The grace was expressed in the form of enlightenment.

It was at night. With a feeling of deep frustration and a sense of defeat, I stood on the lake shore. I saw the moon reflected on the water. As I was watching the moon on the lake, I suddenly came to myself. "Why do I have to worry about the grade? Why did I come to the seminary? I did not come here to get a good grade; I came because God called me." As I reflected to myself, I suddenly felt that I was free from the conventions that kept me away from my true intention. "The F-grade was a grace, not a disgrace. It helped me to rediscover the real purpose of my coming here," I said to myself. After that, I wanted to recognize the teacher as a means of God's grace to me. I changed my attitude completely after this experience. I decided to see him in person and express my thanks and reconcile our enmities.

One day I saw him coming toward me. He tried to avoid me, but I forcefully confronted him and said, "Hello." The word "hello" worked like magic. It melted down the ice that had frozen us. We stood on the sidewalk for a long time and talked as if we were old friends. He told me that he also wanted to say "sorry" for what he did to me. I was so glad that we had reconciled our anger and mistrust. At the commencement he stood beside me and spent more time with me than any other teachers and friends.

It is not easy to be reconciled with someone you hate. But if you try hard, God will give you his grace to overcome the barrier. The experience of reconciliation bestows a joy upon us beyond our ordinary experience. This joy of peace is the beginning of our peace with God. Let us be reconciled with our neighbors before we seek to be reconciled with God! Amen.

16

The Meaning of Thanksgiving Day

By faith Abraham obeyed when he was called to go out to a place which he was to receive as an inheritance; and he went out, not knowing where he was to go. By faith he sojourned in the land of promise, as in a foreign land, living in tents with Isaac and Jacob, heirs with him of the same promise. For he looked forward to the city which has foundations, whose builder and maker is God.

(Hebrews 11:8-10)

It was more than thirty years ago when I first celebrated Thanksgiving Day in the United States. When I first arrived in this country one summer day, I was so busy with the new life and strange phenomena that I had no time to reflect upon myself. The college where I was enrolled started in the fall, and I had no time to give special notice to the change of seasons. The first holiday I had was Thanksgiving Day. I saw that the trees were changing their colors. The fall was so beautiful. I recalled my homeland, where I used to celebrate our Thanksgiving Day with my own family and friends.

In my homeland we used to take the first and best of the harvest from the fields and make rice cookies from it and dedicate them to the ancestral gods. I recalled the journey to different grave sites at Thanksgiving time. This was the traditional custom for celebrating Thanksgiving Day in our homeland. The ancestral worship was one of the most important events in our lives. We thanked our ancestral spirits for the good harvest and the blessed year.

After I became a Christian I gave up ancestor worship. I began to give my thanks to the God who manifested himself through Jesus Christ. I began to understand the real meaning of Thanksgiving, for God is the giver of all things. The family with whom I celebrated my first Thanksgiving Day in this country were also Christians. I still remember the most delicious turkey dinner that we had together. After the meal my American friend tried to explain the meaning of Thanksgiving Day. This was the first time that I came to realize the special meaning of Thanksgiving Day as celebrated in this country. "This is also my first year in this country," I said, identifying myself as a pilgrim. "You are the pioneer of your own people in this country," my friend said. This remark was most profound. I felt at that very moment that I was a pioneer and this new land was my own. Then I gave my most sincere and genuine thanks to God, who gave me this new land. To my friend this land did not mean anything new, but to me it was new. "I am a pioneer in this land," I reaffirmed to myself. The real meaning of Thanksgiving Day for me was to become a pioneer in this land.

As a pioneer to this new land, I thought of Abraham, who left his own homeland after receiving the call of God. He was accompanied by his family when he left his homeland, but I was alone. It was easier for me to adjust in a strange land because I was alone. It must have been extremely difficult for Abraham to adjust in strange places, for he had to take his family with him. I further compared my life with that of Abraham, who had overcome so many difficulties in his journey. My journey was easy compared with Abraham's. I gave thanks to God for this. Abraham left his homeland because of God's call, but I did not receive any call from God.

I came to this land by my own initiative, for my own interest; I wanted to find a better place to live. God promised the new land to Abraham, but he did not promise this one to me. At this point I could no longer identify myself with Abraham. I then became depressed and wondered whether God really wanted me here. I hesitatingly asked my American friend, "Do you really think that God wants me to become a pioneer in this land?" My friend replied with a smile and said, "If you happen to stay here for good, then take it as God's will." This was a most helpful remark for me. It became, in fact, the basis for my theological justification of living in this country. Although I did not hear or know the call of God, I responded to it. Perhaps it was my lack of faith that prevented me from hearing his call.

That is why I began to notice in the Letter to the Hebrews the importance of faith, the faith of Abraham. Without faith, Abraham might not have heard the call of God. It was by faith that he received the call. For me it was for lack of faith that I failed at that time to receive God's call to this new land. Now I have faith to understand his call for me to become a pioneer in this new land. Therefore, the issue was not whether or not God called me to come to live in this new land, but whether or not I had enough faith to hear his call. In other words, it was my faith, not God's call, that mattered the most. Everyone who has faith is called by God to become a pioneer. However, those who are called cannot be pioneers unless they have faith. By faith Abraham became a sojourner, the pioneer of his tribe. By faith he became the ancestor of the Chosen People. Therefore, by faith I can become a sojourner in this new land of America. By faith I can become the pioneer of my own people and be blessed in the same way that Abraham was blessed. By faith I can receive the inheritance of this land and have descendants like the sands of the seashore or the stars in the sky. By faith I have been chosen to become a child of God. That is why the true meaning of Thanksgiving Day is to have faith.

Faith alone helps me identify myself with Abraham. By faith I have endured pain and suffering as a pioneer in this land. The suffering of rejection is one of the most common experiences that has tested my faith in the past thirty years in this country. I have been rejected by many Americans in my role as a pioneer in this land. They have not accepted me as their own companion in my pilgrimage here. They have often treated me as an alien who does not have an inheritance in this land. I have often felt that I was an unwelcome guest in this land.

When I was rejected as a fellow member of my own church, I again questioned God's call to be a pioneer in this land. It was in June of 1961 that I was interviewed by the Board of Ordained Ministry for my admission into full membership in the Annual Conference. At the board meeting I was denied full membership in the conference, because the members of the board felt that the local churches were not interested in having me as their minister. The chairman of the board said: "Once you become a member of our conference, our bishop has a responsibility to appoint you to a local church. However, we feel that no church in our conference is ready to accept you as a minister. I am sorry." When I heard it, I was deeply afflicted with the pain of rejection. I wondered at that time whether God had called me or not. It was my lack of faith that questioned God's call.

With deep frustration and a sense of shame I came out of the conference room and walked all the way to the lakefront. As I was standing alone, mindlessly watching the waves coming all the way in from far away, I suddenly heard a familiar voice. It was my bishop's call. "Jung, would you like to have dinner with us this evening?" It was a surprise. I was also flattered by his invitation.

As I came to the dinner table, there was a bishop from another state beside the wife of my bishop. When we sat down, my bishop introduced me to him, by saying, "This man, having come all the way from Korea, is going to become a full member of our conference." "No. It is not true," I said abruptly, interrupting his introduction. Everyone was stunned when I said it. I explained to him what the Board of Ordained Ministry had decided. When he heard it, my bishop was really concerned for me. He then said: "You must come into our conference. I will take the responsibility for your appointment. Please go and tell the chairman that I want you to be accepted into full membership in our conference." It was a ministration of grace to me. With his assurance my face began to shine. My faith revived. By faith I had overcome my humiliation and shame. By faith God gave me the grace to transform a sense of rejection into the assurance of acceptance into the fellowship of the church. I gave thanks to God for his grace. The day that I was accepted into full membership in the conference was my Thanksgiving Day.

By faith the strange land becomes my homeland and the alien country becomes my own. It is not faith in the nation but faith in God, who is the creator and owner of all things. God is the owner of this land, and anyone who believes in him as his Father can inherit this land. I have come to possess that faith to believe that I have inherited this land from my Father. America is no longer a strange country to me, because I am a Christian, and this land belongs to my Father.

When I was a boy in Korea, I used to go on picnics with other students. One day we went about fifteen miles away from home to a famous mountain, known as the Mount of the Merciful Mother (Chamo-san). On its top were several houses. An old gentleman was kind enough to guide our group into the castle, which was built in earlier days to defend the country from foreign invasion. I was curious to know who could own a huge mountain like this, so I asked him. He said, "Everything in this area used to belong to Lee Kun-su." The name was so familiar that I was deeply puzzled. Suddenly, I recalled my grandfather, whose name was the same. I said,

"My grandfather was also Lee Kun-su." When he heard me, he asked me where I came from. I told him everything about my father and my town. He then held my hand like an old friend and said, "Oh, my boy, all these mountains and surroundings used to be your grandfather's land." When my friends heard him, they looked up to me like to a prince. I was filled with joy. I began to look around with a new perspective. Everything seemed intimate and affectionate toward me. There was no sense of strangeness. I felt that the land and mountain were mine. I developed an affection for that land.

Likewise, when I came to believe in God as my Father, this land of America was no longer strange to me. It is my Father's land, and I have inherited it from him. I feel comfortable in the land where my Father called me to come. This is my land, just as it is the land of others who believe in God. That is why by faith I love this land and take care of it as if it were my own.

When Abraham came to the place where God had promised him, he built an altar as a token of his thanksgiving. I also want to build a church. That is why I have a Korean Christian Fellowship, which meets every week to worship God. This is my response to God's gift of this land. By faith I take everything as God's gift to me. My life is also his gift as well. When I come to realize that everything is his gift, then every day becomes the day of thanksgiving. This seems to me to be the true meaning of Thanksgiving Day. Thanks to God, who gives me faith to accept all things as his gift. Amen.

17

The New Ethics of Jesus

*Y*ou *have heard that it was said,
'An eye for an eye and a tooth for a tooth.' But I say to you, Do not
resist one who is evil. But if any one strikes you on the right cheek,
turn to him the other also; and if any one would sue you and take
your coat, let him have your cloak as well; and if any one forces you
to go one mile, go with him two miles. Give to him who begs from
you, and do not refuse him who would borrow from you. You have
heard that it was said, 'You shall love your neighbor and hate your
enemy.' But I say to you, Love your enemies and pray for those who
persecute you, so that you may be sons of your Father who is in
heaven; for he makes his sun rise on the evil and on the good, and
sends rain on the just and on the unjust. For if you love those who
love you, what reward have you? Do not even the tax collectors do
the same? And if you salute only your brethren, what more are you
doing than others? . . . You, therefore, must be perfect, as your
heavenly Father is perfect."*

(Matthew 5:38-48)

It is important for us as Christians to remind ourselves that
the ethics that Jesus taught in the New Testament is different
from that which we usually practice in this society in our daily
lives. We practice the ethics of retaliation and retribution, but
the ethics of Jesus is that of unconditional love. What we
practice in our society is the ethics of justice, but the teaching

of Jesus is based on the ethics of love. That is why we as Christians have to remind ourselves of what the new ethics of Jesus is, to which we should adhere in our lives. This new ethics seems to be differentiated into three stages of evolvement: The first stage is the renunciation of the traditional ethics of retaliation, the second is the ethics of yielding, and the final stage is that of unconditional love. The ethics of unconditional love leads toward Christian perfection.

First of all, Jesus repudiates the traditional ethics of justice. He introduces the phrase, "But I say to you," as a way of repudiating the ethics of retaliation. The traditional ethics of retaliation is to extract "an eye for an eye and a tooth for a tooth." This is the ethics of justice. If someone picks your eye, you pick his eye in return; and if he knocks out your tooth, you also extract his tooth. In this way, justice is restored. Our civil law is based on this kind of ethics. If someone kills my children, I expect him to be killed in the same way. If someone steals some property, he is expected to return the same amount or to receive a penalty equivalent to the amount. This kind of ethics is based on justice. If someone hits you, you hit him back. We build our lives around the ethics of retaliation. Therefore, many of us teach our children to fight back. Moreover, we want to see our government retaliate against those who support terrorist groups. Jesus, however, renounced this kind of retaliation.

Why did Jesus renounce the ethics of retaliation? What is wrong with an ethics based on justice? Jesus did not tell us why the Old Testament ethic of retaliation is wrong. However, it is really quite clear why he repudiated it. First of all, the ethics of retaliation creates more problems than solutions. Let us take an example from our family living to illustrate the principle. If a wife commits an extramarital sex act and the husband in retribution goes out and commits a similar extramarital act, this will create still more problems in the family. Let us take another example. When your wife is angry at you, you may also express your anger at her in return. However, this will create more intensive anger between the two of you.

Another reason that the ethics of retaliation is not acceptable is that, in retaliating, we place ourselves on the same moral level as the evildoers. In other words, we have to put ourselves in the same moral position as those against whom we retaliate. We believe in Christ because we want to be better persons. Therefore, as Christians we cannot follow the ethics of retaliation. Finally, the reason we as Christians reject such an ethic is that we believe in the just God, who alone has the prerogative to retaliate against evil. "Vengeance is mine, says the Lord." Retaliation belongs to God. Therefore, Jesus introduces a new morality based upon love rather than justice.

The new ethics that Jesus taught is that of yielding to evil. He said, "Do not resist one who is evil." But if any one strikes you on the right cheek, turn to him the other also." By yielding to evil acts, one can overcome the evil. Some may wonder how evil can be overcome by their yielding to it. How can the kingdom of righteousness be established, we may ask, by yielding to evil? Of course, this is more than just an act of non-violence. Jesus' method is that of yielding. If an evil person takes away our coat, we not only let him have it but we also offer him more; we give him our overcoat, too. If an authority requisitions us to carry a heavy load for a mile, we should not stop there but should go another mile for him, too. But are we not helping him in his unfairness, we may ask, by giving more than he asks from us? How can we overcome the evil by yielding to it?

Before we try to answer these questions, let us examine the life of Jesus. Jesus practiced what he taught; he did more than what his enemies wanted from him. You may well remember what Jesus did when Judas was going to betray him. He not only allowed Judas to do so but also urged or hastened him to do it, saying, "Do [it] quickly." Here, Jesus went further than what Judas wanted. Jesus assisted him in carrying out his plan of handing Jesus over to the Roman soldiers. Even at the time of his trial, Jesus never resisted but yielded himself even to death. Why did he practice the method of yielding?

I know why Jesus used this method; it is because yielding is the most powerful means to overcome an enemy in love. The method of yielding is stronger and better than the method of retaliation, even though it is more difficult to practice. Let me illustrate it with my own experience in my youth. When I was in primary school in Korea, I was known as one of the best wrestlers in my class. When we had a wrestling contest, even though I was rather short in comparison with other classmates, I ended up the match wrestling with the strongest one in the class. I learned the way of yielding, which is also known as the Way of Tao. I used to yield myself all the way to the enemy, so that I could use his own power to defeat him. In other words, I learned to yield myself so totally that I was no longer differentiated from him. Because of this he had to fight for himself. When he finally exhausted himself, I was ready to use my own reserves of strength to defeat him.

Since one of the best examples to illustrate the power of yielding is water, this became the symbol used by the Taoist philosophers. Water does not react to the rock; rather it circumvents the rock by yielding. Nevertheless, the water eventually overcomes the rock. In other words, by yielding, the water finally wears the rock away. There is also a Korean proverb that can be used to illustrate the power of yielding. It says, "If you hate him, give him one more ricecake." Ricecake was regarded as an unusually precious food in the early days. The proverb means that we should be nicer to those whom we dislike. It is smilar to what Jesus said: "If any one forces you to go one mile, go with him two miles." Doing more than what the enemy wants, we can make the enemy repent and change to become our friend.

Let me also share another experience with you. When I first started to teach, I reacted negatively to students who disliked my teaching or were condescending toward me because of my Oriental background. My reaction to their attitude created trouble in my teaching. Thus I learned that the ethics of retaliation did not work. Therefore, I tried the ethics of yielding. I began to pay more attention to those who disliked me; I gave them favors that they did not deserve. And eventually, they came to like me after all. From my own experience, I learned that, while the ethics of retaliation creates more problems, the ethics of yielding resolves problems by transcending the conflicts. It can reconcile wounds and heal them. Thus, Jesus taught the ethics of yielding as a means of transforming evil into good.

The new ethics of Jesus is also that of unconditional love, which was in fact his central teaching. "Love your enemies and pray for those who persecute you," he said. Over against the ethics of hate and retribution, Jesus taught the ethics of unconditional love. Loving enemies and praying for those who persecute us is the most difficult task of humanity. It is a love that transcends yielding. It is a love that gives unconditionally. It is by his love that God gave himself for sinners like us. Such love is not possible for us alone, but is possible for God. It is possible for us if God be with us. What Jesus commands is that we extend this unconditional love to others. This is the finest form of ethics that we know. However, it is also an impossible ethic for those who rely on their own power. The unconditional love of our enemy is possible only to those who embody sainthood. It was Mahatma Ghandi who, when he was assassinated by the bullet of his enemy, placed his hand on his forehead as a sign of forgiveness. To forgive one's own persecutor or one's own assassin is not an ordinary act; it must be classed as a saintly

115

act. Ghandi followed the teaching of Jesus, who taught us to love the enemy. Jesus also practiced it in his life: He died for those who persecuted him, and he forgave them, for they did not know what they were doing. This is what Jesus asked us to do. It is not possible with our own strength, but it is possible with God.

The ethics of unconditional love finally leads us toward Christian perfection. "You, therefore, must be perfect, as your heavenly Father is perfect." This is the goal of every Christian. God commands us to be perfect, perfect in love. Many are familiar with the doctrine of perfection, with perfect love, with the love that goes beyond our own power. Although this may be a goal rather than an actuality, we ought to pursue it, drawing upon the power of God's grace.

The mark of a Christian is that he or she practices the new ethics of Jesus. Caught up in a world where the ethics of justice is practiced, the Christian finds it is a hard task to practice the ethics of unconditional love; yet we are called to practice such love in this world. In the midst of a society of retribution and retaliation, one who would experience the bearing of the cross must practice the method of yielding. Yielding to evil is a mark not of defeat but of the eventual victory of love. Christ yielded to the uttermost, giving even his own life for the evils of this world. We as followers of Christ must learn to love our enemies and pray for those who persecute us. This is the real challenge of being Christians in our time. This challenge is too much for us to meet with our own meager powers of response, but is not impossible when God's love is within us. May the power of such love be in us all. Amen.

18

A Perfect Gift

*T*he angel said to her, *"Don't be afraid, Mary; God has been gracious to you. You will become pregnant and give birth to a son, and you will name him Jesus."*
(Luke 1:30, 32 GNB)

We have a tendency to relate Christmas to the receiving and giving of gifts. We know that the real meaning of Christmas is more than the exchanging of gifts, but we are often forced to follow the mood of our time. In the world of our materialistic and consumer-oriented society, we attempt to create the mood of Christmas by doing what we know best; that is, by substituting material for spiritual gifts to express our thanks and love for one another. Our church has attempted to persuade the congregation to change their attitudes and make Christmas more spiritual. Nevertheless, any real progress that is being made toward the new way of celebrating Christmas is all too slow. Perhaps one way to reorient people toward a more meaningful expression of Christmas might be to imbue them with a new understanding of what a "gift" is. Christmas has a deep and intrinsic connection with the gift, the perfect gift, that we receive. The real problem with us, however, is not the idea of gift, but the kind of gift that we want to receive or give.

What we need at Christmastime is a perfect gift, and for

this reason we spend much time and energy looking for it. For most people Christmas is not a joyous season, not a peaceful season; instead, it is one of the busiest seasons of the year. People are busy looking for perfect gifts for their loved ones. As parents of children, they have to spend a great deal of time at stores and on the streets looking for perfect gifts for their children. Stores are busy during this season earning a good fraction of their profits for the year. It is the time for businesses to exploit the psychology of children and youth. Every producer of merchandise tells us that his goods will make the perfect gift. We have trouble in selecting what is the perfect gift for ourselves and for others.

What is it that makes a gift perfect? Most people believe that a perfect gift is one that perfectly meets the desires of the one who receives it. In other words, the perfect gift is that which the receiver wants to get. Therefore, the common practice in our time is to ask our children to list the items that they want to get at Christmas. As parents you may have done exactly what I have to do at Christmas. We have to take the list of items that our children want with us when we go to the shopping center. Often we have to hurry to get just what they want. And that is why we begin to shop right after the Thanksgiving holiday is over. Especially in a small and remote town like ours, it is almost impossible to get everything we want unless we begin our shopping early.

Although we spend many hours and days finding perfect gifts for our children, we do not succeed. Year after year, Christmas morning turns out to be something less than what we had hoped for. We have spent so much time in finding perfect gifts for the children that we are completely exhausted by the time the day arrives. Our energy and time were mostly spent in looking for the gifts that the children want. Therefore, there is little time left in which to prepare mentally and spiritually for making Christmas Eve or Christmas morning more meaningful.

There have been many occasions in our home when Christmas was one of the most miserable days in our lives. The reason was that we could not find perfect gifts for our children. Usually when Christmas morning comes, our children come to the Christmas tree and find their gifts. Just like other families, we ask our children to open their gifts one by one. One of the reasons parents do this, no doubt, is that they want to give satisfaction to their children. Since our children have already indicated what they want to have at Christmastime, they are happy when they unwrap the things that they wanted. However, if they do not find the things that they wanted, they are frustrated and Christmas morning then becomes a miserable time. No matter how hard we try, sometimes we cannot find everything that they want. I remember some years ago when we bought everything that our children wanted except one item, which was not available. My children were quite upset because of this one item. That Christmas day turned out to be a miserable one.

Even if we were to find everything that our children wanted, we would simply be providing what they have already expected to receive and nothing surprising or exciting would occur. Therefore, Christmas Day will turn out to be dull and meaningless if we think of Christmas merely as a time of receiving and giving gifts.

After all, the material gifts that we want cannot be perfect gifts. A perfect gift must bring joy, happiness, and a grateful heart. If we cannot find joy at Christmastime, we have not found the perfect gift. The perfect gift must make us happy, not miserable; peaceful, not frustrated; and grateful, not obnoxious. But, if what we want does not make the perfect gift, what does make the perfect gift at Christmas?

The perfect gift is possible only to those who do not expect to receive. The problem with us is that we expect to get gifts at Christmas. Our expectation or desire to receive limits the kind of gifts that we can receive. The limitation is imposed by

119

ourselves. This means that we cannot have more than what we can expect. Since we are not perfect ourselves, what we want cannot be perfect either; it cannot be a perfect gift. The perfect gift, then, is possible only when we expect nothing. This means that the perfect gift has to be a surprise. However expensive and important a gift might be, it cannot be a perfect one unless the one who receives it is surprised by it.

The first Christmas gift that I received when I was a boy was a pair of socks. It was a real surprise to me, because this was the first time that I had received anything at all on Christmas. Of course, most people in our town at that time did not know what Christmas was. But my mother was a Christian, so my father decided to observe Christmas day. This tiny gift filled my heart with joy and gladness because I did not expect anything. It was not the quality or the quantity of the gift that I received, but my attitude that made the gift perfect. However perfect the gift might be, it cannot be a perfect gift unless it is a surprise. What makes the gift perfect, then, is not the gift itself; it is the emptiness of heart or the poorness in heart of the recipient that makes the gift perfect.

The most perfect gift we receive at Christmas is not one of our gifts but God's gift to us. This is the gift of God's Son, the baby Jesus Christ. Those who had expected to receive God's Son could not receive him; that is, the Jews who expected to receive the Messiah did not receive Christ as the Messiah. For them Jesus was not the perfect one. Because they expected what they wanted—that is, one who could restore the Davidic Kingdom of Israel—the perfect gift of God, Jesus Christ, was not the perfect gift for them. However, those who did not expect to have the Messiah received the perfect one. They were mostly Gentiles, oppressed people, or simple shepherds, who accepted Christ as a surprise.

Christ comes to us as the perfect gift at Christmastime when we are free from the preoccupations and anticipations of our own wishes and desires. Christmas is a time to empty our hearts, so that we can receive the perfect gift from God. If we fill ourselves up with our own gifts, we may not find room for God's perfect gift. The city of Bethlehem could not empty a room for Jesus, but our city should be able to provide an empty room for him. The perfect gift that God gives us can perfect us. That is why it is perfect. It is also a lasting gift. Other gifts that we receive at Christmastime are short-lived. However precious and expensive the gifts might be, they can offer only temporary satisfaction. But the gift of God is eternal.

Let us not try to find perfect gifts at Christmas. We will never find them. Let us accept the perfect One, who comes to us only when we are truly free from our own wishes and greed. Let the perfect gift become our surprise at Christmas. The real meaning of Christmas is to receive the perfect gift of God and to render our joy and thanks to him. Help us empty our heart and make us be the poor in heart, so that we may receive the perfect gift at Christmas. Amen.

19

Seed

It is like a grain of mustard seed, which, when sown upon the ground, is the smallest of all the seeds on earth; yet when it is sown it grows up and becomes the greatest of all shrubs, and puts forth large branches, so that the birds of the air can make nests in its shade."

(Mark 4:31-32)

A farmer knows the importance of good seed. When seeds are not good, they do not germinate. Moreover, we cannot expect a good harvest when the seeds are poor. Therefore, the most important thing that the farmer has to consider is the selection of good seed for his fields. No matter how much time we spend laboring to raise the crops, we cannot expect a good result in farming unless we begin with good seeds. However rich the soil might be, it cannot produce anything good unless the seeds are good.

Since I grew up in a small farming town, I know how important seeds are for farming. My parents used to sort out the best of the crops when the harvest was done; and until the seeds for the next spring's planting were separated out, the crops were not consumed. The seeds were kept carefully separate from the other crops. By selecting the best seeds for the next year's planting, we were able to maintain the quality of the crops at their highest level.

The importance of seeds reflects the significance of beginnings. The seed implies the beginning. Everything seems to have its beginning, which implies that everything has its seed. Every great work begins with a seed of thought. For Jesus, the seed here means the Word of God, which marks the beginning of our new life. As we notice in the parable of the sower, the seed, or the word of God, is the beginning of the Kingdom of God (Matthew 13:3b-9). The Word has to be proclaimed first, so that the kingdom of God may come on earth. The urgency of proclaiming the Word marks the importance of the beginning of the coming kingdom. The spreading of the Word of God is none other than the scattering of the seeds across the soil.

The seed as the Word of God also represents Christ himself. The Gospel of John begins with the Word, which is identified with Christ, the Son of God. It was the Word which came into the world. This, then, is the meaning of the incarnation of God in human form. Thus, the seed as the Word of God is more than just the written words of the Bible; it is Christ himself, who came to dwell in our hearts. Our new life begins with the presence of Christ within us. When the seed is sown in us, it begins to germinate and grow within us. The seed that represents Christ is certainly a good seed and is, indeed, the perfect seed.

The seed contains the future potentiality of its becoming. It contains implicitly all of the textures, forms, colors, and sizes of the plant that it represents. One of my interests is to plant the seeds of fruits that I like. After tasting the fruit, I take out the seed from it and plant it in a pot. When I plant the seed, all I know about it is the fruit; I do not have any idea about the plant. Only when it starts to grow do I begin to see the plant that I have never envisioned before. It is a revelation to watch the unfolding of the mysterious potential hidden in a tiny seed. The size of the seed does not tell us the size of the plant that eventually evolves. A small seed, in fact, may often contain the potential for making a huge plant. The future possibility is hidden in the seed.

Likewise, the Word of God contains all the potential for future greatness. Like the seed, it contains the blueprint for the future kingdom of God. In it, God's plan of salvation is already implicit. It has the dimension of eternity, where the end and the beginning meet. Thus, the Word of God as the seed contains what the world is and will be. Nothing can be added to or subtracted from what is already implied in the Word of God. We cannot alter the divine plan of salvation, which is crystallized in the Word of God. What we can do is to promote the divine plan, just as we can help the seed to germinate and grow, for the actualization of its potentiality. We can plant the seed and give it water, so that God will make it grow. For God is the ruler, and we are his servants.

The seed not only contains the potentiality of future becoming, but it also has the power to realize its potentiality. The greatness of the Word of God as the seed in the parable of Jesus is the power of actualization inherent in its potentiality. The potentiality alone is not enough; the Word of God as Christ has also the power of self-realization. In Mark 4:26-32, we notice that the seed has the intrinsic power to realize itself when all the conditions are met. When the seed is planted in the soil, it grows if light and water are provided. When we compare the Word of God with the seed, we understand why the Word of God has the power of self-realization. What makes the seed grow is none other than the power of God the Creator. Therefore, the Word of God is none other than the incarnation of God; it has its own power for self-actualization.

We see the self-actualizing power of the Word of God when we look at the creation story in the book of Genesis. The creative power of God is manifested in his Word. In the story of creation, God uses his Word to create everything. "Let there be light," God said when he created the light. He did not use his hand to create it; rather, he used his Word as a means of creation. Likewise, he said, "Let there be water," and so forth. Here, we can notice that the creative power is in the Word. The Word of God is creative, for it is God in manifestation. Just as the seed contains the power for self-realization, the Word of God has the creative power for the plan of God.

This seed of creative power for the transformation of the world lies in no other place than within our own heart. The preaching of the Word is for the purpose of making us realize the presence of the Word of God within us. By hearing the Word, we realize the inner presence of the Word of God. Therefore, our faith in God begins with our hearing of the Word, though the presence of God within us does not begin with the preaching. God was with us, in fact, and is with us from the beginning to the end of the world. This means that the Word of God, which represents the Son of God, has been with us, although we have been unaware of his presence. The presence of this transforming power within us is the greatest gift of God. Many people do not realize this power as a gift and attribute it to themselves or to some other deities.

What I am trying to affirm here is sacramentalism, the belief in the presence of the spirit in all things. The spirit, which has been regarded as a hidden power, is known under many different names. The basic definition of religion, as coined by the founder of cultural anthropology, Sir Edward Tyler, is to believe in the spiritual presence in all things. This animistic definition is widely espoused in most Third World countries, where Christianity is not regarded as the dominant religion. A good example of this kind of belief is shamanism, which is still regarded as the native religion of the Korean people. The shamanist believes that the spirit is the most powerful force present in all things. Especially, it is the presence of the spirit that generates not only the blessings but also the ills of the living. Most shamanistic rituals have been aimed to please the spirits who are in control of human destinies. The spirit, to the shamanist, is a creative power very closely related to the idea of the seed. Anything that happens to us is in one way or another dependent upon the spirit. If we possess the good spirit or the good seed, we are blessed and our future will be bright; however, if the spirit is not good, then misfortune will befall us. In this way shamanism appeals to the spirit as the dominating force of human life.

When we think of the presence of the Word of God in man, however, we are not suggesting the shamanistic idea of a spiritual presence within us. The Word of God is none other than God himself in the form of flesh (Christ) and of his Holy Spirit. The shamanistic idea of spiritual presence is very closely associated with the biblical view of "principalities and powers" (Ephesians 6:12), which have been regarded as the enemies of Christ. The presence of the Word in us is the actual presence of God, who is over all things and the source of all spiritual and physical existence. The seed that is implied in the teaching of Jesus is not the spirit in any ordinary sense; it is the Word of God who is present in us. It is then the indwelling Christ who becomes the archetype of our existence. As the seed is the basis for the plant, so the Word of God is the basis for humanity. What we can become is dependent on the Word of God, for the Word is the inner essence of our existence. We are then compelled to say that the essence of our being is the Christ, the archetype of all humanity.

This idea is very closely related to the Confucian notion of *Jen* or the essential goodness of human nature. According to Confucianism, the basic nature of a human being is good, so that evil is a distortion of the original goodness in man. This idea is often regarded as contrary to the Christian notion of original sin, according to which human nature is intrinsically evil. However, the intrinsic nature of a human being must be traced back to times before the Fall; the essence of humanity then was good. Christ, therefore, is identified as the second Adam, the true humanity as it was before the Fall. The idea of the indwelling Christ or that of the seed helps us reinstate the inherent goodness of human nature. If Christ is our archetype, we must trace our origin to him, just as the origin of the plant must be traced from its seed.

The seed or the Word of God in us is small. It is compared to the mustard seed, the tiniest seed known in the time of Jesus. The Word of God in us is smaller than the smallest; it is, therefore, invisible. Yet it contains a potentiality greater than the greatest. Just as the tiniest mustard seed becomes the greatest tree, so also the Word of God can expand God's kingdom beyond the scope of our imagination. We are witnesses of that expansion and instruments of God's creative force at work in the world. Therefore, in the final analysis, God is all in all. This is the significance of the seed in our lives. The seed is the Word of God, which is in us, and has the power to grow and transform our lives. May it grow fully in us, so that we can say, as Paul did, "It is no longer I who live, but Christ who lives in me" (Galatians 2:20). Let us praise the God who gives us the seed for our lives. Amen.

20

The Weeds

*L*et both grow together until the
harvest; and at harvest time I will tell the reapers, Gather the weeds
first and bind them in bundles to be burned, but gather the wheat
into my barn."

(Matthew 13:30)

This parable of the weed is a continuation of the parable of
the seed. The good seed represents the Son of God or the
Word of God in the flesh; and the weeds signify the children
of evil. The parable of the weeds makes no attempt to solve
the problem of evil in the world. Rather, it helps us take the
problem of evil seriously. The actual existence of evil is
affirmed. According to this parable, evil seems to be a part of
God's original design. In other words, God does not want to
remove evil from the world; he wants evil to co-exist with
good. This does not mean, however, that God likes evil. He
hates evil and likes good. But in order to save good, evil has to
be retained. Evil is included in good, and good is in evil.
Therefore, the destruction of evil would eventually destroy
the good as well. Since they are interdependent, one cannot
be sorted out from the other. What the parable attempts to say
to us is that we have both good and evil in our lives; that we
cannot have good without evil; that at the end of the time,
however, God will judge between the good and the evil. Just

as the wheat is separated from the weeds, so also will the good be saved and the evil thrown into hell at the end of time.

Why does God allow the weeds or evils to exist in the world? Why did he create the evils if he is good? If God really loves us, how can he allow the evil to create so much suffering in the world? Many questions are prompted by the parable of the weeds. Some theologians attempt to answer the questions, the questions of theodicy, by saying that evil is only a shadow, or non-being, and thus only an illusion. If evil is non-being, however, then it is not real. But the parable of the weeds definitely affirms the existence of evil, the reality of misfortune and malevolence. The weeds are real; they are not illusions.

We know the existence of evil in the world; we have experienced it many times. One of the most unforgettable memories I have of the Korean War is that of a child clinging to his mother who had died in the bombing. The child did not understand that she was wounded by the bomb and had died. The crying sound of that child still rings in my ears. How could God, the loving God, have allowed this innocent child to suffer from the loss of his mother? Besides such manmade evils, there are also natural disasters such as earthquakes. Thousands of people were buried in 1985 under the rubble of buildings in Mexico City. How can the loving and almighty God allow such innocent ones to suffer by wars, famines, and natural disasters? No one has found a really satisfactory answer to these question. Many theologians and intellectuals have left the church and even given up their faith in God because of the problem of evil in the world. When we carefully reflect upon Jesus' parable, however, we may find something worthy of consideration on the existence of evil in the world.

In this parable of the weeds, we notice that the weeds have to be kept alive for the sake of the wheat. While God does not love the weeds, they do have to be left to grow together with the wheat until the time of harvest. This seems to imply that evil is necessary for the preservation of the good. In other words, in order to keep the good and save it from harm, the evil has to be kept too. In the parable, the weeds are not to be pulled out because the wheat might be uprooted as well. God then keeps the evil because he loves the good and wants to keep it unharmed.

The coexistence of good and evil suggests that the world that God has created is not perfect and not yet completed. The creative process is still continuing toward its consummation. We are living in an incomplete world. God is indeed the Creator, but he is still creating through processes that lead toward completion. That is why Jesus said that his Father is still working. His creative work is not yet finished. When the world is perfected, then evil and disorder may disappear from the world. To me this is the meaning of the appeal, "Thy kingdom come . . . on earth as it is in heaven."

Although natural disasters and the sufferings of the innocent may reflect the imperfection of the world in which we live, most evils exist owing to the freedom of humanity. What makes humans different from other creatures is their freedom to choose between good and evil. This is the moral quality uniquely attributable to human beings. In Oriental thinking, heaven represents the spiritual quality, earth the material quality, and human beings the moral quality. What makes humans different from other creatures is their morality. Where there is nothing but good, humans cannot make a moral choice. But one who cannot make a moral choice is less than human. Therefore, for the sake of people's authentic existence as human beings, the coexistence of good and evil would seem to be essential. Moreover, a person cannot appreciate the goodness of God without evil, just as one cannot appreciate joy without the suffering in the world. Thus, the coexistence of good and evil seems to make sense.

From the parable we can also notice that the real

distinction between good and evil or between the wheat and the weeds is not discernible until they grow up and bear their grain. They look alike when they are mere shoots. Since I grew up on a small farm, I understand the parable of weeds. Unless one is an experienced farmer, one has trouble in the beginning in differentiating the wheat from the weeds. A clear distinction between them is possible to make only when they bear their grains. Therefore, the final separation between them must be made at the time of the harvest.

The ultimate judgment between good and evil comes from God. He is the one who can sort out the weeds from the wheat. God's wisdom is sharper than the edge of a knife. It can discriminate between the good and the evil. " 'Vengeance is mine,' says the Lord." God alone is the final judge. Having made the separation, God first orders that the weeds be bound together to be burned, and then that the wheat be gathered into the barn. In other words, the evil ones are condemned to hell, and the good ones saved and brought into the kingdom of heaven. Although the evil ones may enjoy life, they will be punished at the end. On the other hand, the good ones may suffer in life, but they will find eternal joy at the end of the world.

One of the powerful symbols that has motivated many people to become good is the image of hell. Although it represents a negative approach to moral teaching, the fear of eternal hell has played an important part in *awakening* the conscience of the people. I still remember the horrible picture of hell depicted on the streetcar when I was in Seoul. A hell with burning fire was the message displayed for unbelievers. In the parable of the weeds, a vivid picture of hell is drawn, with the furnace of fire into which the evil ones were thrown. The torment of the evil ones, weeping and gnashing their teeth, was perhaps the basis for the picture of hell that was drawn and placed on the streetcar. Here, fear of the final judgment is clearly stated. "The fear of the Lord is the beginning of wisdom" (Proverbs 9:10). There is no love and respect without justice and fear. The love of God includes both acceptance and judgment. God bears a two-edged sword—one edge for love and the other for judgment. God loves the good, but he judges the evil ones at the end.

Let us become the wheat, not the weeds. By its fruit the wheat is distinguished from the weeds. The wheat bears good seeds for the kingdom, but the weeds produce the evil seeds of the world. The weeds grow faster than the wheat and are stronger than the wheat. Likewise, it is easier for us to do evil than to do right. The way to righteousness is narrow and hard, but the way to evil is wide and easy. Therefore, let us take up the armor of Christ and fight against the evil forces around us. Let not the weeds take us over. May God give us his grace to overcome evil and endure until the end. Amen.

21

The World Is My Parish

*Go therefore and make disciples of
all nations, baptizing them in the name of the Father and of the Son
and of the Holy Spirit, teaching them to observe all that I have
commanded you; and lo, I am with you always, to the close of the
age.*"

(Matthew 28:19-20)

"The world is my parish," said John Wesley, the founder
of Methodism. This should be our motto, reflecting the basic
characteristics of our church.

In the past, Methodists have had a tendency to boast of the
structural uniqueness of their church. We are still proud of
our connectional structure, but our stress should not be
placed upon structural or methodological matters. This is a
misplacement of priorities. Methodology is secondary, for it
is merely a means for effectively dealing with issues and
problems. Our prior concern should be the vision of the true
Church, which the risen Christ commissioned us to witness
to and proclaim. "Go into all the world," said the risen
Christ, "and preach the gospel to the whole creation" (Mark
16:15). The mission of the Church is none other than to
follow this commission. "The world is my parish" is then our
church's response to this commission.

First of all, the mission of the Church presupposes the

presence of the risen Christ in the world. What makes the presence of the risen Christ different from that of the earthly Jesus before death? Certainly, the presence of the risen Christ is not a denial of the presence of the earthly Christ, for the former is the fulfillment of the latter. The presence of the risen Christ transforms the earthly Christ into new and universal dimensions.

The earthly Jesus lived within the confines of space and time, but the risen Christ transcends these limitations. The risen Christ is present everywhere and all the time. He is present in many different places simultaneously, for he is the manifestation of the Spirit. Because he is present everywhere in the world, the whole world is our parish. The Church is everywhere at all times. For as Jesus said, "Lo, I am with you always, to the close of the age."

The presence of the risen Christ makes the Church truly inclusive. The earthly Jesus was a Jew, but the risen Christ is a cosmic reality. He is no longer confined by a specific race. He can manifest himself as a Chinese to the Chinese people, a black person to the black people, a white person to the white people, and an Indian to the Indian people. The same Christ can manifest himself in different forms and different colors. The earthly Jesus was a male, but the risen Christ transcends sexual distinctions. Because the risen Christ is present in spirit, he transcends all categories of thinking: all sexual distinction, all racial difference, and all cultural and traditional norms. Since the presence of the risen Christ is spiritual and inclusive of all things, the Church where this presence is realized has to be universal and inclusive. The church that is not inclusive and universal cannot be an embodiment of the true Church.

One of the serious mistakes that the early missionaries made was their failure to recognize the inclusive presence of the risen Christ in the world. They depicted Jesus as a white Anglo-American male and brought that picture to the Asian and African countries. When I was a boy, all the pictures of Jesus that I saw along the streets of Seoul were of a white man. I knew why people used to call Christianity the religion of the white man. Later I came to realize that the earthly Jesus was not an Anglo-American, he was a Jew, who probably had dark skin, black hair, and brown eyes. However, the risen Christ manifested himself as a European to the Europeans. The same Christ could have manifested himself as a Korean to the Korean people and as an African to the African people. Therefore, it was a mistake for the early missionaries to bring the white Jesus to Asia and Africa. The risen Christ is the cosmic Christ, who transforms all earthly things into cosmic dimensions. Therefore, the Church founded on the presence of the risen Christ is universal and inclusive. "The world is my parish" is, then, the vision that Wesley had in reflecting upon the universal presence of the risen Christ in the world.

Second, the risen Christ is the real missionary, and we are his disciples. In spite of the presence of the risen Christ in our midst, we have tended to act as if he were not with us, as if the Christ had not risen from the dead. We have acted as if he had left us never to return again. We have therefore made ourselves the representatives or the deputies of Christ. We have made ourselves his agents in order to act on his behalf in his absence. We have acted as if God can do nothing unless we do it ourselves. We have to take everything into our own hands, because we think that Christ is no longer in control.

Because we have acted as if the risen Christ is no longer with us, we also take responsibility for all that we have done. If the church loses membership, we have to blame ourselves. If the church gains in membership, we take the credit for it. The success or failure of our ministry is then considered to be totally dependent on our own effort, through which we have made the church into a business organization and the ministry into a profession. We have come to depend more on psychology than on prayer, more on reason than on faith, more on our own work than on God's grace, and more on structural efficiency than on the spiritual power of God.

By acting as if the risen Christ were not present in us, we have persecuted him. In general, ignoring someone's presence is the subtlest form of discrimination. I have often been treated as if I did not exist. People have acted and talked in front of me as if I were not there. It was a painful experience to know that my existence meant nothing to them. I have experienced this because I am yellow and a minority in this country. The presence of the risen Christ, however, is ignored by us because he is invisible. Through our ignorance he is ignored. By ignoring his presence among us, we persecuted him, as we did the earthly Jesus.

If we think that we ourselves control our church, the living Christ becomes a captive, a prisoner in his own house. When the master is locked up within his own house, the assistant is then free to act as an agent on behalf of his master. Is the living Christ locked up in your church? Have you chained him in with your logic, confined him with your structure, and dismissed his presence because he is invisible? I hope that this is not happening in your church today.

What is needed is to recognize that Christ is alive. He is present among us. However, sheer recognition is not enough; we must act on the belief that he is with us. This act is faith. This faith, by which we act on his presence, has the power to heal the sick and transform the world.

When our action becomes our response to the presence of the living Christ, we can no longer act as his agents; instead, we become his disciples and assistants. We can no longer act on his behalf, for he too is present himself as the real missionary. We become his helpers, and our study and our work then serve to assist him in his mission. Even in our theological training we must learn how to serve and assist the living Christ, rather than to direct and manage the church on behalf of Christ.

As his servants we must direct our best efforts to assist him to act in his own way. If we do our best, it is enough. We need not worry about consequences. If the work happens to be successful, the credit should be given to Christ and not to us. If it fails, we deserve no blame. However, God never fails if we let him work in us and through us.

Finally, to become the disciples of the living Christ means to follow him, which means, in turn, to yield our priorities to him. It means to make him the master of our lives, to let him occupy the center of our lives! It means, as Paul said, that "it is no longer I who live, but Christ who lives in me" (Galatians 2:20). The recognition of the indwelling Christ is not enough; we must experience it, just as Wesley experienced it at Aldersgate. The experience of Christ's indwelling then becomes the power that compels us to preach the Good News. The Good News is that Christ is not only raised from the dead but is with us today. Just as Mary Magdalene was compelled to tell the news of the risen Christ to the disciples, so also we ought to be compelled to tell people of the presence of the risen Christ in the world. "Christ is with us" is the Good News that we must proclaim and witness. Let the world know that the Christ is present. This is the essence of what Wesley meant when he said, "The world is my parish."

Countless people in the past felt compelled to witness the presence of Christ and died for it. Among them is a man who was special to me and to other Koreans. He was Henry Appenzeller, the first Methodist missionary to Korea. He was in his late twenties when he arrived in Korea on Easter Sunday, April 6, 1885. He felt compelled to tell the good news to everyone. His favorite passage was Romans 1:16: "For I am not ashamed of the gospel: it is the power of God for salvation to everyone who has faith, to the Jew first and

139

also to the Greek." After several years of service in Korea, he returned to America for his first year of sabbatical leave. He was then only in his mid-thirties; but he already had the marks of age, with gray hairs all over his head. Though his friends advised him to stay in America, he returned again to Korea. After another several years of service he came back to America for another sabbatical year. At that time, when only in his early forties, he was already an old man. His face was so wrinkled that no vitality was left; there was only dry skin. He was so weak and fragile that his friends tried to stop him from returning to Korea, saying, "You are too weak now. You are going to die there. Please stay here with us." But Appenzeller asked, "What difference does it make where I die? Is it easier for me to get to heaven if I die in America?" He returned to Korea for the third time. A few months later he was on his way to Mokpo, taking two high school girls and a laywoman with him in a steamboat. The boat collided with a large merchant ship. At that time Appenzeller was in a first class room at the top of the boat, a position from which he could easily have been transferred into the merchant ship before it was too late. Instead, he went all the way down under the deck to rescue the girls and the woman, who were in a third-class room. By the time they were brought up to the deck, it was too late to get off the boat. Appenzeller died with them.

His death was a loss, but also a gain. Out of his death Christ came to live in the hearts of the Korean people. Look at the miraculous growth of the church in Korea: every day six new churches are started. Ten years ago only 10 percent of the Korean population were Christians; now 20 percent are Christians. If the growth continues at the same speed, by 1990, 30 percent will be, and by the year 2000 half of all Koreans will be Christians. That means that we will have 150 million Christians within the fifteen years. Moreover, the largest congregation in the world is located in Korea. This is a miracle. No man can do this; it is the work of the risen Christ, who lives and acts in the lives of the Korean people.

What then is happening to our churches in this country that sent the first missionary to Korea? Is our United Methodist Church dying? We lose members every year. Have we reached old age? Like a living organism, the church that does not grow will eventually die. What is happening to our church? Have we lost the vision that Wesley had? Have we lost our faith in God, who can do all things? Have we forgotten the presence of the risen Christ in our midst? Or have we tried to build the Kingdom by our own image? Money is important, buildings are important, knowledge is important, structure is important; but what God values in us most is our heart. Does our heart sense the presence of the living Christ? Is the risen Christ living in our midst? Are we compelled to witness to the world that Christ is present? Unless our hearts are warmed again by the presence of the risen Christ, our church cannot revive. Let us recapture the vision of Wesley that "the world is my parish." Let us all own the living Christ to be the master in our lives, and let God be God! Amen.